Beachhouses 2

Beachhouses 2

STEPHEN CRAFTI

Published in Australia in 2003 by
The Images Publishing Group Pty Ltd
ABN 89 059 734 431
6 Bastow Place, Mulgrave, Victoria, 3170, Australia
Telephone: +61 3 9561 5544 Facsimile: +61 3 9561 4860
Email: books@images.com.au
Website: www.imagespublishinggroup.com

Copyright © The Images Publishing Group Pty Ltd

The Images Publishing Group Reference Number: 512

All rights reserved. Apart from any fair dealing for the purposes of private study, research, criticism or review or as permitted under the Copyright Act, no part of this publication may be reproduced, stored in a retrieval system or transmitted in any form, means, electronic, mechanical, photocopying, recording or otherwise, without the permission of the publisher.

National Library of Australia Cataloguing-in-Publication data

Crafti, Stephen
Beach Houses 2

ISBN 1 876 907 95 9

1. Vacation homes – Australia. 2. Vacation homes – New Zealand. I. Title.
II. Title. Beach Houses 2

728.72

Coordinating Editor: Sarah Noal

Designed by the Graphic Image Studio Pty Ltd, Mulgrave, Australia
in association with Design Corp, Melbourne, Australia.

Film by Ocean Graphic Company Limited

Printed by Max Production Printing & Book-binding Limited

IMAGES has included on its website a page for special notices in relation to this and our other publications. It includes updates in relation to the information printed in our books. Please visit this site: www.imagespublishinggroup.com

Contents

10   Preface

BEACH HOUSES

14   A Beacon
18   Moving on from the Past
22   A Deliberate Orchestration
24   The End of a Journey
28   Worth the Climb
32   A Small Footprint with a Large Impact
34   Like Driftwood
38   Among the Trees
40   A Panoramic View
44   Nestled into the Bush
48   A Contrast of Styles
50   A Landmark
54   One Form
56   A Series of Boxes
60   A Sense of Scale
62   An Impressive Swathe
66   Casuarina Beach House
70   Two Sides
72   The Original Footprint
76   Anchored to the Landscape
78   Above the Dunes
82   Sculptural Form
86   A Tropical Retreat
88   The Highest Point
92   Once a Cottage
94   A Sense of Performance
98   The Full Brunt of the Weather
102   Wedged in

Contents continued

104	Leaving the Suburbs Behind
108	Opening to the Views
110	Sharing Time
114	A Large Viewing Platform
118	Manipulating the Site
120	Sharing the View
124	Maximum Exposure
126	About the Landscape
130	A Small Village
134	Protection from the Wind
136	A New Form
140	180-Degree Views
142	Out to Sea
146	A Roof with a View
150	Great Escape
152	A Sense of Rhythm
156	Robust
158	An Unexpected Space
162	A Sustainable Approach
166	A New Edge
168	A Sense of Enclosure
172	A Horizontal Band
174	A Journey
178	Through the Back Door
180	Strategic Incisions
184	On a Crest
186	Featured Architects
192	Acknowledgments

Preface
BY STEPHEN CRAFTI

The coast has always been a source of inspiration for architects. Far removed from the hectic pace of city life, coastal retreats offer a chance to reflect on the natural elements, the sea, the sand and the bushland.

Away from the constraints placed by local councils, neighbours and the community, the beach house offers both the architect and client the opportunity to realise their visions. Evocative of a farmhouse experienced as a child, one beach house featured in this book realised the client's dreams. Another, resembling an old-fashioned camera, is carefully angled in its bushland setting. And another beach house, taking the form of a simple crate, is sensitively worked into its coastal environment. Many of the beach houses, shown here, hang precariously over their bushland escarpments. Others are deeply entrenched in the native scrub, only making their presence felt once one has entered through the front door. In impressive coastal surroundings, these beach houses offer unique glimpses of some of our finest contemporary architecture.

These beach houses are exposed to the elements. The sand from the beach forms a trail to their entrances and becomes a continual addition to the living room floor. The wind, often blustery on the coast, is also considered via well-designed and protected courtyards and patios. And replacing the sound of traffic is the sound of the waves on the shoreline. Featuring large glass sliding doors, many of these beach houses bring these coastal conditions to the heart of their living spaces.

Whether glass and steel, or timber and stone, these beach houses also explore materials not normally considered for use in the city. Like the texture of the sand, many of these beach houses have a tactile quality. A soaring 'ramble stone' fireplace is as much a feature as the weathered bark on towering gum trees. Another beach house, featuring a textured curved concrete spine wall, invites caressing as well as exploring. But whether the beach house is made from concrete, stone, glass or timber (or all of these materials combined), there is a sense of spontaneity in each design.

As the trend to living in smaller spaces, such as high-rise apartments, increases worldwide, so does the desire to escape to a beach house on the weekend. From a simple timber structure with rudimentary services, to elaborate architect-designed homes, the beach house continues to offer an important sanctuary. And, like the breathtaking coastal environments in which they are located, the memory of these houses lingers on the journey back to the city.

BEACH HOUSES

A Beacon

ROBERT PULLAR OF ARTICHOKE DESIGN STUDIOS
Photography by Allan Chawner

From a distance, this beach house appears to have landed from another galaxy. Constructed in compressed fibro-cement sheeting, the unpainted surfaces include exposed bolts. "The house had to be as maintenance-free as possible (which included a zinc-clad roof). It's a salty environment. The materials chosen had to stand up to this corrosive environment," says architect Robert Pullar, who designed and also built this house.

Tightly framed by neighbouring homes, the architect was keen to create the feeling of being in a more remote location. Consequently, many of the conventional side windows were substituted for irregular-shaped glass panes with views towards the surf and the sky. Essentially the two-storey house takes the form of a square. It is only the roof and the building's upper façade that is angled 45 degrees. To accentuate these dramatic angles, Pullar also designed an angular timber deck to spill over into the grounds. "You could say the house looks like a large oyster, particularly when you're sitting on the terrace (leading from the main bedroom)," he says. Left in its natural grey colour, the fibro sheeting certainly suggests the shell of an oyster.

In contrast to the protective lip of the upstairs terrace, the main living area below provides a continuous vista to the ocean ahead. "I didn't want to include any columns on the terrace. They would have dissected the views," says Pullar. While the more exposed aspect of the site can be appreciated from the living room sofa, a deck behind the kitchen provides a more sheltered environment. Pullar also designed a separate pavilion-like garage and guest wing (facing the street) to protect the home's central courtyard from the prevailing winds. "The children, grandchildren or guests can have their own space. The pavilion occupies roughly the same space as the original house on the site."

Colour, both internally and externally is a feature of the house. The base of the buildings were rendered and painted in purple and green, reflecting the Bougainvillea that grows on the property. The vibrant internal colours also provide a sense of freedom from the more restrained colour palette used in city homes. As Pullar says, "At night the colours appear to glow. They provide a beacon when you're walking along the beach at night."

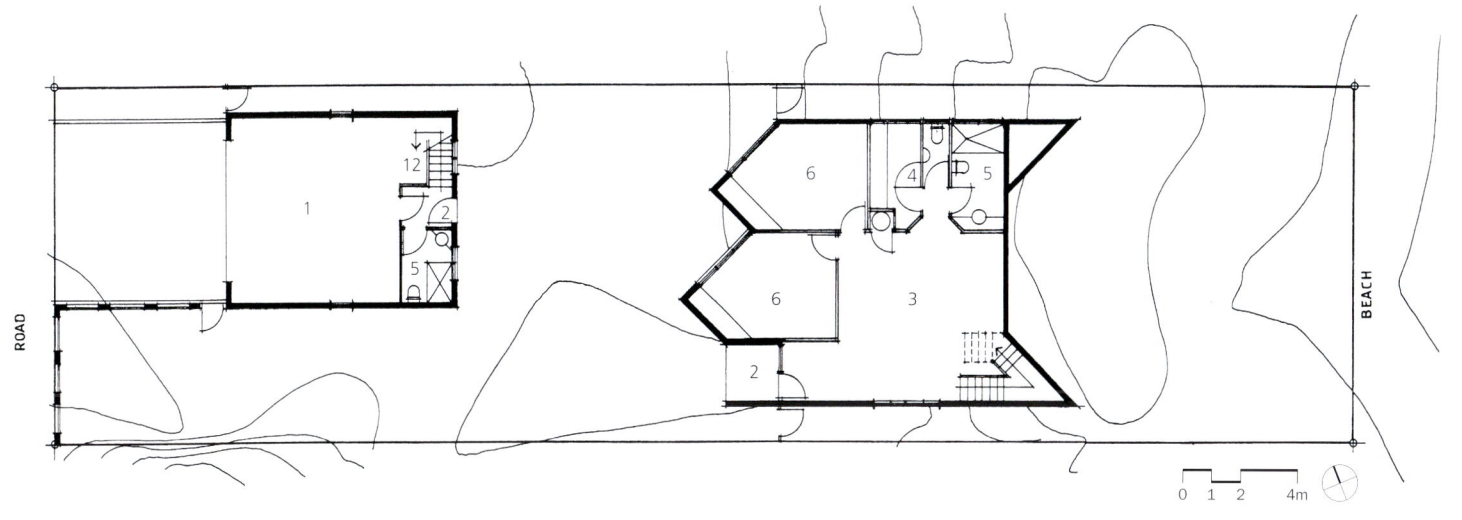

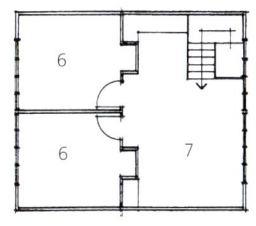
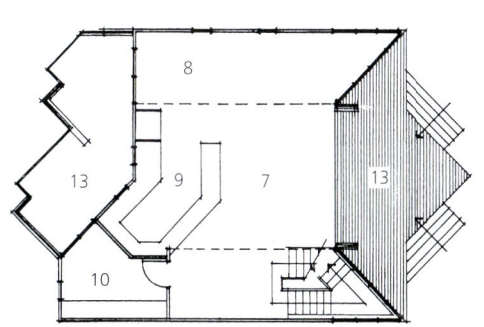

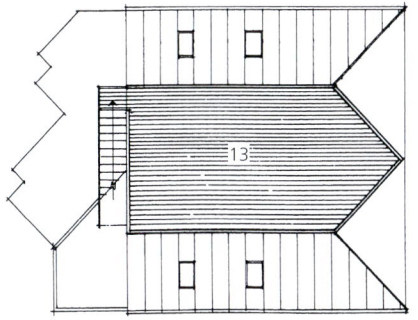
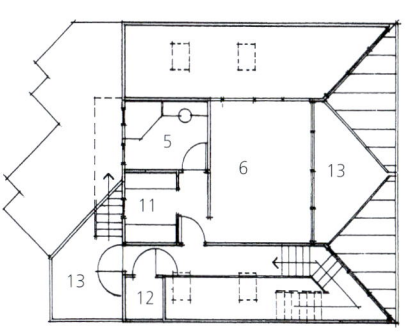

1 Garage
2 Entry
3 Billiards
4 Laundry
5 Bathroom
6 Bedroom
7 Living
8 Dining
9 Kitchen
10 Study
11 Dressing
12 Store
13 Deck

Moving on from the Past

VALDIS MACENS ARCHITECTS

Photography by Brett Boardman

This cliff top used to be scattered with weatherboard cottages. While many have been cleared to make way for new homes, this new house, designed by Valdis Macens Architects, incorporates the original Edwardian-style cottage, built at the turn of last century.

The cottage sits on top of the cliff face, with the new contemporary levels on two lower levels. Built on a sandstone base, the new home features sandstone as a plinth in the design. "The sandstone was quarried from the site," says architect Valdis Macens. "My clients wanted a weekender that could also be used as a family home down the track. The brief was fairly open, but they wanted to include a protective courtyard from the breezes and somewhere to retreat from the summer heat," he says.

The weatherboard cottage was reworked. What was once the verandah to the cottage is now a sunroom, accessed by three bedrooms. The entire cottage acts as a separate wing for the children. While there is direct access from the cottage to the new house on the lower levels, a forecourt on the middle level provides the main access point. The entry also provides a new sheltered area for the owners.

The new areas of the house are not only defined by large glass windows, but also by the shape of the ceiling. The kitchen, for example, is defined by a vault-shaped corrugated steel roof and the adjacent living/dining wing has a pitched roof. "The original building was defined by holes in the wall. The new spaces are more like a series of pavilions," says Macens.

A main bedroom, ensuite, and study were designed on the lowest level of the house. With the children's wing in the cottage, and the parent's wing at the bottom of the cliff face, the kitchen and living areas in between act as a buffer zone. Alternatively, the home offers accommodation for two families who want to operate independently of each other. While privacy in the house wasn't difficult to achieve, creating a sense of seclusion from neighbouring homes required significant skill. "It's a fairly dense area. We didn't want the neighbouring homes to distract from the magical views ahead."

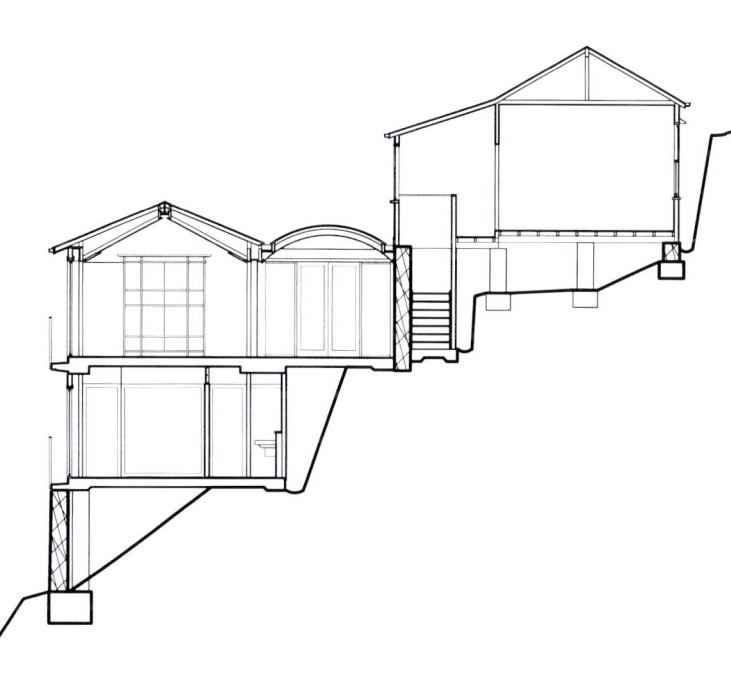

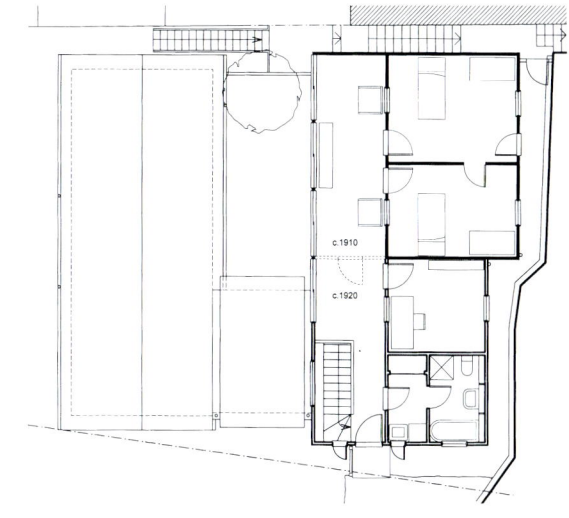

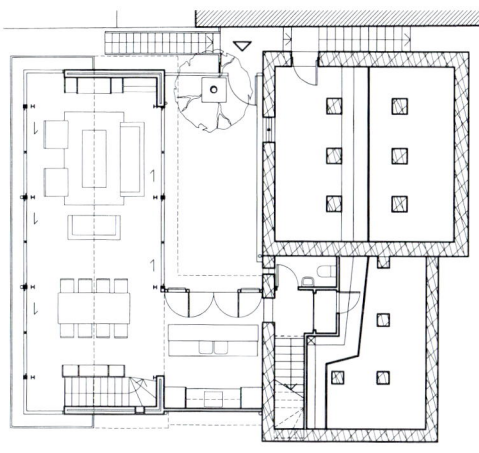
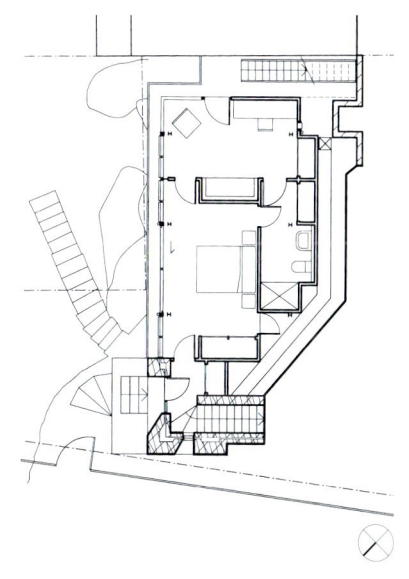

A Deliberate Orchestration

DALE JONES-EVANS ARCHITECTS

Photography by Ashley Jones-Evans and by Stephen Blakeney

A generous triangular site overlooking the ocean was the perfect stimulus for a die-hard surfer to build his dream home. "My client was looking specifically for the 'Bombie' (a surf term for the premier wave spot)," says architect Dale Jones-Evans who designed this extraordinary new house.

Accessed via a cul-de-sac, the site unfolds over a 25 per cent gradient and has a 360-degree view of the Indian Ocean. While Jones-Evans could have designed a house with views that provided instant gratification, he preferred to set up a journey where the experiences gradually unfolded. There were a number of significant elements in the landscape. "There's the strong ridgeline of the landscape. It's almost like a floral sea. There's literally the sea and the crashing surf and also an intriguing church that was built in the 1950s, which forms an outcrop in the landscape." Each element is slowly discovered.

A small aperture in the home's front elevation (facing the cul-de-sac) is accessed via a banded horizontal path. Tucked in behind rendered walls, which act as a barrier to the prevailing winds, the entrance to the home is cave-like. "It's like entering a citadel. You can't see around the building. It's a bunker that follows the contours of the land." The 'bunker' contains the bedrooms and bathrooms, while the lighter component, the floating copper dome, includes the kitchen, living and outdoor areas. "There are two opposite sensations of 'bunkering into' and 'floating over' the landscape. The building is designed to age and crust, the cement render will soften and leech salt and the copper will oxidise green," says Jones-Evans.

Through a narrow slot in the kitchen wall there is a glimpse of what lies ahead. Standing in the kitchen, the picture unfolds, with the ridgeline and sky to one side, views of the church to the other. To ensure that the finishes do not distract from the design, Jones-Evans used concrete for the kitchen floors and for the terraces either side. Even the kitchen bench was designed in concrete. "It's like one giant brushstroke," he says.

The copper roof, which made the house a beacon in the area, was literally pulled down from 2.8 metres at the centre of the living area, to 2.1 metres at the edge. With the lowered ceilings, there's a cave-like experience when either entering the home or moving out onto its expansive patio. At the tip of the building, on the cantilevered patio, the entire landscape wraps around the house.

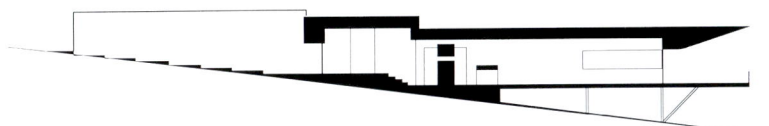

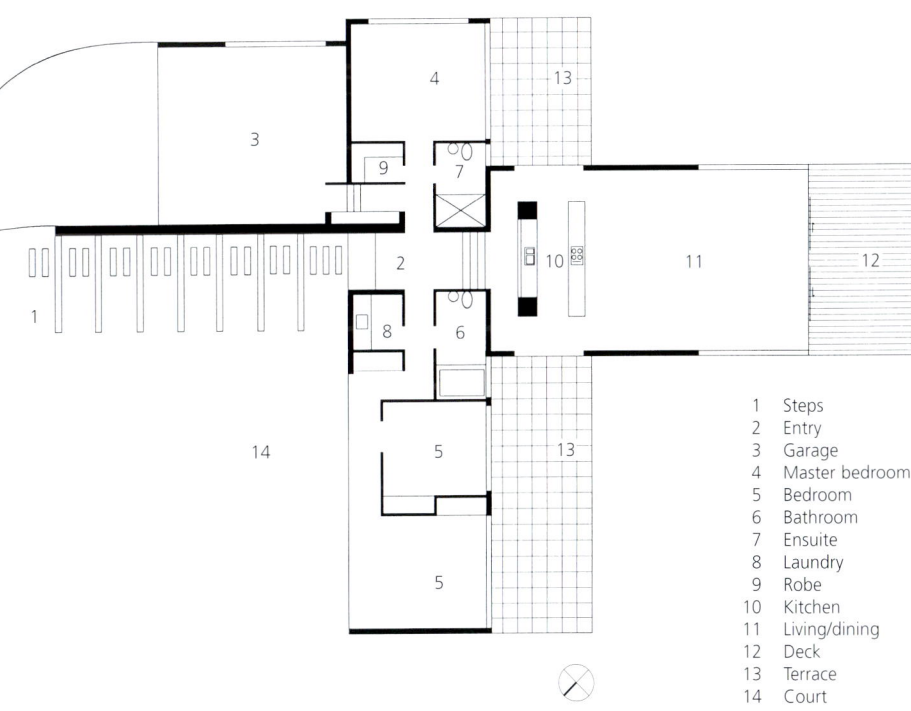

1 Steps
2 Entry
3 Garage
4 Master bedroom
5 Bedroom
6 Bathroom
7 Ensuite
8 Laundry
9 Robe
10 Kitchen
11 Living/dining
12 Deck
13 Terrace
14 Court

The End of a Journey

DAVID LUCK ARCHITECT

Photography by Earl Carter

Architect David Luck had the idea for this weekender for a number of years. "I sketch up ideas as they come to me," says Luck, who often mounts his schemes in poster-sized frames on his office walls. "The site immediately suggested this design." In black and mossy fossil green, this new house looks more like an old-fashioned camera waiting to capture its next image.

While not large (approximately 10 square metres), the home focuses on the coastal bushland through large picture windows and doors. "The house was designed as a lookout at the end of the journey," Luck says. Across a walkway and through a large glass front door, the colours of the bush create a striking image. Reflecting the colours of the tree trunks, the blacks, charcoals and greens are interrupted only by the colour of bright red sap occasionally dripping from the bark.

Designed on a gradient of 10 per cent, the angled internal ramp follows the slope of the site to a number of pod-like rooms. They are opened to each other and carefully angled to the views and the light, so that there are few divisions in this home. The main bedroom, with a mosquito net enclosing the bed, is defined only by a change in floor level and yellow-tongue flooring contrasted against the black ramp. "On warmer nights, the door is left open, hence the net to keep the mosquitoes out," says Luck. Banquette-style seating was originally planned for the kitchen but the view to the bush was considered more important. The alcove is now an additional space for the leisurely reading of newspapers and magazines.

In the kitchen, an 8-metre laminate bench acts as both the kitchen and dining room table. Enclosed in a glass box, the kitchen's fragility is emphasised by the external guy wires (used on telegraph poles) anchoring the structure to the ground. As the internal walls in the house had no cross bracing, the steel wires protect the structure from strong winds. The main living area was designed as one large outdoor deck. Surrounded by full-length glass doors, the living area can be opened up during the warmer months. In winter, the focus is towards the potbelly heater.

The house, made of BHP Colorbond steel, is elevated above the terrain and is sensitive to its unique bushland setting. From the road, it is difficult to identify the house. It could easily be just another charred tree trunk.

This house first appeared in Domain, in *The Age* newspaper.

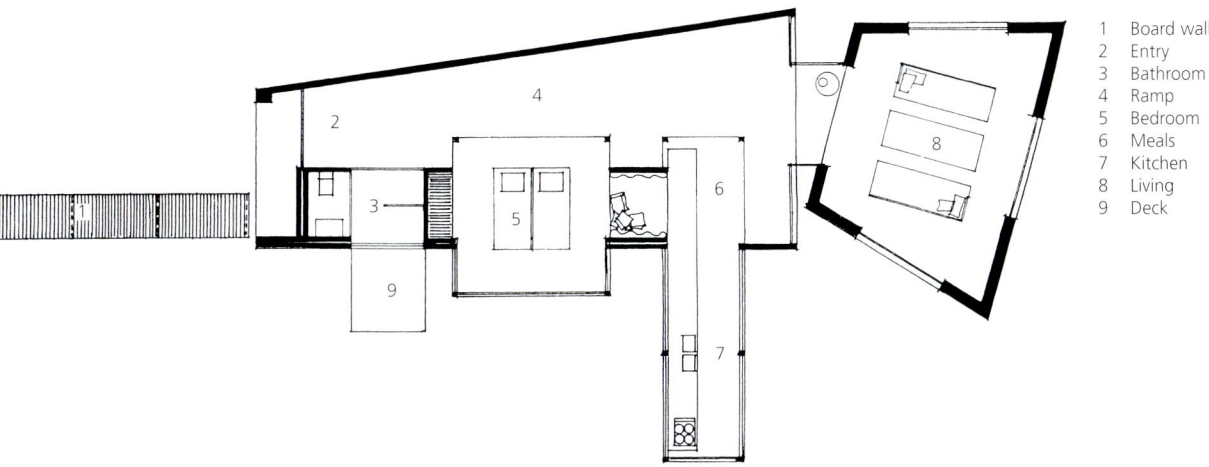

1 Board walk
2 Entry
3 Bathroom
4 Ramp
5 Bedroom
6 Meals
7 Kitchen
8 Living
9 Deck

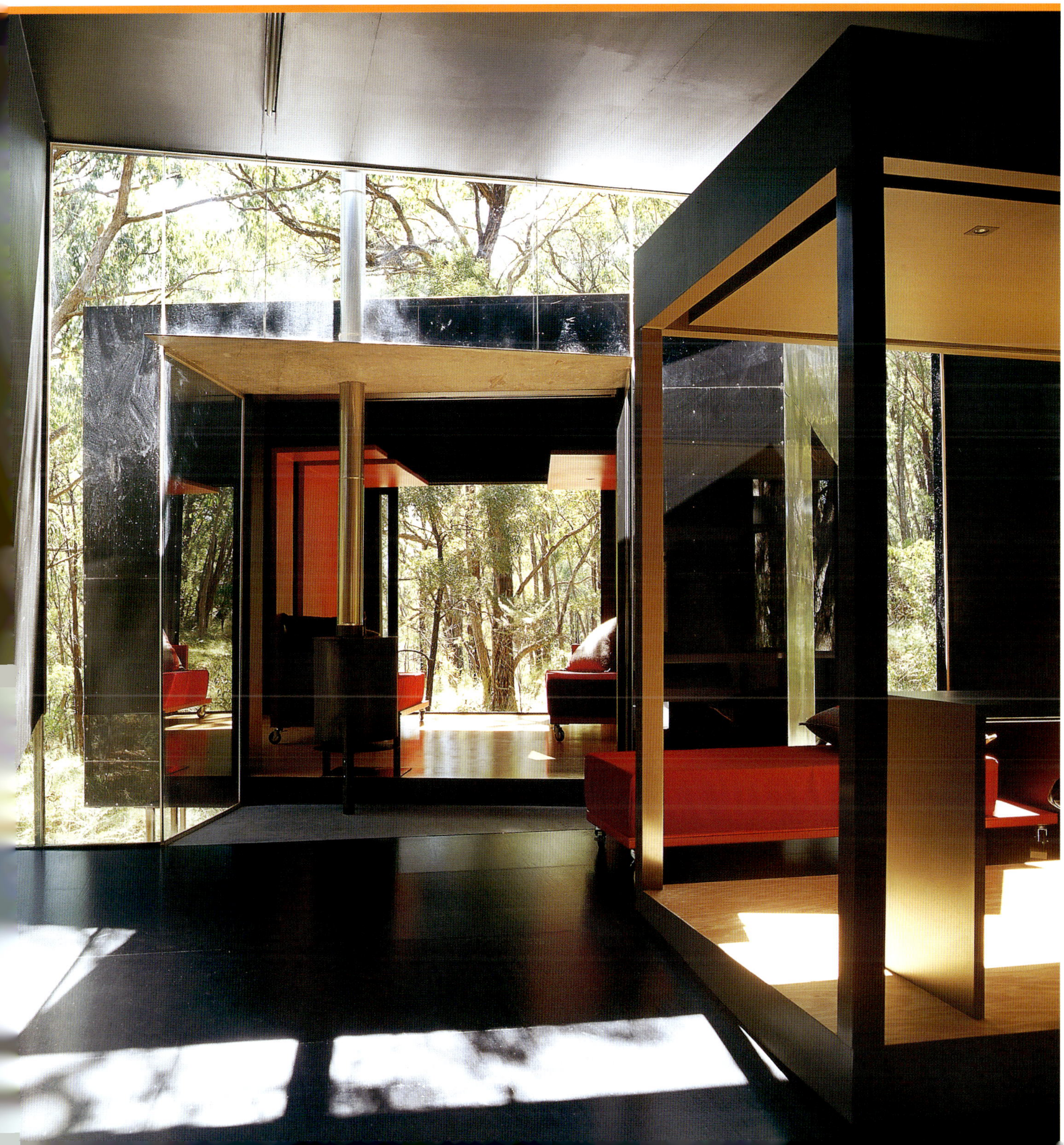

Worth the Climb

ROBERT PULLAR OF ARTICHOKE DESIGN STUDIOS

Photography by Allan Chawner

Overlooking a bay, this beach house was designed for a couple wanting a spiritual retreat. "They wanted a house where they could meditate and relax," says architect Robert Pullar of Artichoke Design Studios.

Located on a steep site, with a gradient of 25 degrees, the architect looked to many spiritual retreats around the world that required a similar ascent, such as Mt. Athos, a monastery in Greece and the Potala in Tibet. "Many of the villages you find in Santorini (Greece) can only be accessed by an endless number of stairs," says Pullar. For this home, Pullar included numerous stairs to connect the three levels. There are 60 stairs between the garage and the main living area on the second level. A further 15 stairs need to be climbed to reach the three bedrooms and bathroom facilities on the top level.

The long narrow site also influenced the design of the fibro-cement and rendered brick home. The main footprint was deliberately angled from the side boundaries to attract the maximum amount of sunlight and to increase privacy from neighbouring homes. Even the large terrace, outside the dining room, is irregular in shape, complete with an angled canopy. "Once the walls were angled, there was the opportunity to create interesting nooks and highlight windows," says Pullar. To ensure that there was one continuous uninterrupted view over the bay, large timber/glass doors framing the dining area can be fully concertinaed. The built-in barbeque on the terrace allows for alfresco dining on warmer evenings. The dining room table can be pulled out onto the terrace. Alternatively, meals can simply be enjoyed from the built-in seating created as part of the concrete-block rendered plinth.

The higher one moves through the house, the lighter the structure becomes. To allow for parking, the site was heavily excavated. The rendered walls of the garage act as the plinth to the home. The first floor is suspended concrete and the top floor was designed with timber floors. The covered triangular timber verandah accentuates the lightness of the upper level. "I wanted to design an open breezeway to connect the bedrooms. It's covered by a translucent sheet which also allows the light to filter down to the lower level," says Pullar.

While many beach houses 'touch the earth lightly', this three-storey house is securely anchored on the site. Though there is a considerable mount to reach the top level, the views are worth the climb. As Pullar says, "There are places to meditate on the way."

1 Garage
2 Courtyard/terrace
3 Dining
4 Sitting
5 Library
6 Laundry
7 Pantry
8 Kitchen
9 Bedroom
10 Bathroom
11 Balcony

A Small Footprint with a Large Impact

DONOVAN HILL ARCHITECTS

Photography by Patrick Bingham-Hall and by Jon Linkins

Known by the locals as the 'T' house, this simple yet extraordinary home, is a landmark in its small beachside settlement. Essentially an 8-by-8-by-8-metre cube, the architect's intention was to keep as much of the natural bushland intact as possible. Surrounded by national park, the landscape is relatively unstructured and undisturbed. "Centralising the activity and accommodation into a single 'box' ensures that the site boundaries can remain indistinct as the local vegetation converges on the building," says architect Timothy Hill of the practice Donovan Hill Architects, who designed this house.

The design centres on a double-height outdoor room. The doors can be closed so that the room can be used throughout the year, rather than only during the warmer months. Instead of solid masonry walls dividing the outdoor room from the bedrooms and living areas, the architects used translucent partitions. The natural light and shadows created by the partitions are quite dramatic, particularly during the summer months.

The timber house is designed over three levels, with entry from the dune into the house's mid-level. The undercroft level is for vehicles, energy services and storage. Entry gates to the living level open directly into the double-height outdoor room. The living level also includes the kitchen and bathroom. The upper level provides the main sleeping accommodation. In this house, the architects designed compact built-in bed cubicles that enable the spaces to be used during the daytime. "We wanted to give the rooms a 'person-sized' appeal and for the owners to have the pleasure of sleeping near the landscape (individual hopper windows were designed at each sleeping platform)."

Even in the outdoor room, there are protected nooks for those wanting some solitude. And surrounded by the native bushland, all the elements can be experienced first-hand. As Hill says, "There are no surfaced roads or drainage services. The areas' character is largely a product of its 'undevelopment.'"

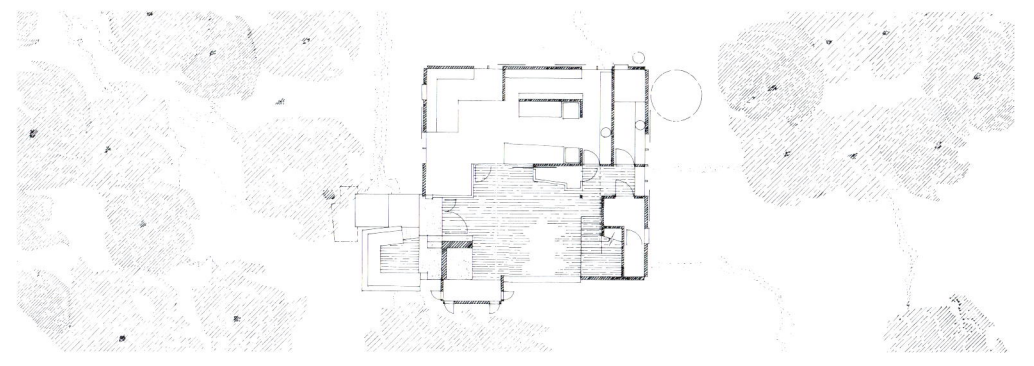
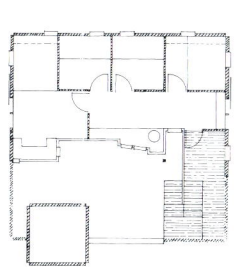

Like Driftwood

CRAWFORD ARCHITECTS
Photography by Martin Van der Wal

This beach house is a 20-minute drive from the main highway. Isolated from passing traffic, the surf-lined coast is largely only appreciated by the locals. But when architect Stacey Jones of Crawford Architects was returning to the city, he made a slight detour. "He immediately put a 100-dollar deposit on a block of land nestled in the sand dunes," says architect John Crawford, who is a co-director of the practice, and whose family are now joint owners of the beachside property.

The two adjacent sites were also for sale. Purchased by people with a similar aesthetic and respect for the sensitive coastal environment, Crawford Architects were commissioned to design three beach houses (including their own). "It's a cliché, but we were all keen 'to touch the earth lightly,'" says Crawford. The three houses, similar in configuration and size, appear to have been scattered on the beach, like driftwood. Clad in western red cedar, which has been allowed to weather naturally, each house has extensive outdoor living spaces framed by 100-year-old wharf timbers. Sliding permeable screens provide privacy when required and protection from the salt-laden sea breezes. A shade cloth above the deck eliminates the harsher summer conditions.

The architects were keen to incorporate the clients' individual requirements using similar materials and forms. "We wanted them to appear as one cohesive group rather than three houses competing to obtain the best views and light," says Crawford. Each house, of approximately 200 square metres, includes generous living areas (approximately 8 by 8 metres). The Jones/Crawford house (shared by the partners' two families) includes a bedroom upstairs and a main bedroom with ensuite on the second level. "We wanted to include a third bedroom above the garage in case guests stay over."

Unlike many of the homes in this beach-house community, these houses appear quite raw. "Some of the locals don't even consider these 'proper' houses," says Crawford. However, unlike many of the permanent residences, these homes require very little maintenance. "The timber has become grey with the weather and there's a real affinity with the elements." When the wind picks up, the screens can be manipulated, fully opened or closed. As Crawford says, "When you are designing a house down here, you really need to be conscious of where the weather comes from. But even when it's overcast, it's still pleasurable being here."

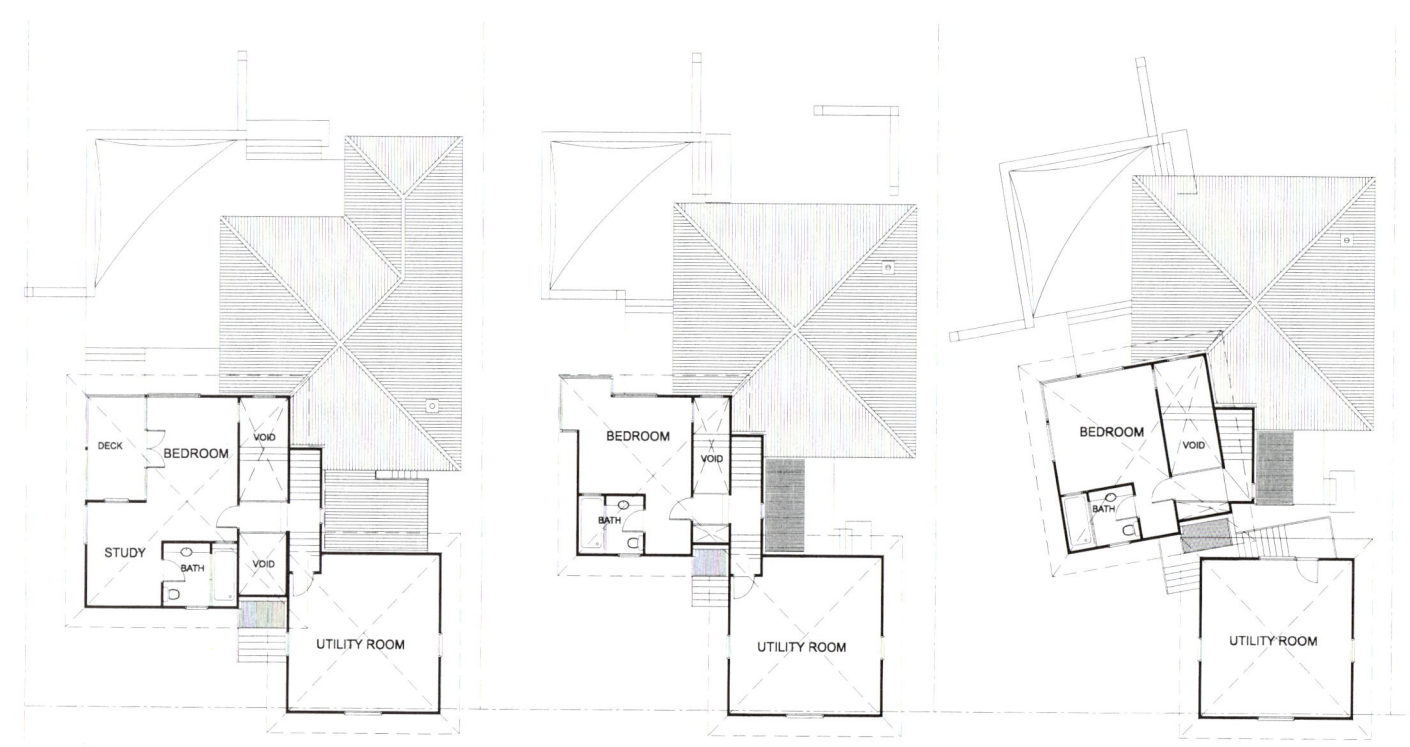

Among the Trees

EDMISTON JONES ARCHITECTS
Photography by Peter Rae

Designed by Edmiston Jones Architects, the owners of this house, a stone's throw from the beach, wanted a simple weekender. "They wanted a weekender with their retirement in the near future. It was a modest budget and they were after a simple house," says architect Brandt Noack, of Edmiston Jones.

Located on a reasonably steep slope and surrounded by other weekenders, the site abuts a reserve to the rear. While the land had been cleared, there was a dry gully on the site that the owners were keen to rejuvenate with ferns. The carport, storage and laundry were located below the house and the architects made the entrance on the first floor, via a semi-enclosed circular staircase. "It's a fairly transparent approach (with timber-batten enclosed walls). The effect is similar to entering a shade house, where ferns are grown under controlled conditions," says Noack.

The house consists of three bedrooms, an open-plan lounge, dining and kitchen area, with bathroom facilities between. "The budget was driving the design to an extent," says Noack. Materials were chosen for their cost-effectiveness – prefabricated frames and timber trusses, prefabricated Masonite cladding and a steel Colorbond roof. The house is set up on a platform and the windows were designed to screen the neighbouring homes and focus on the trees. "It's quite a built-up area. We wanted to create the feeling of being away from everything. It's only when you walk towards the front gate that you're aware of other people in the area," he says.

Originally, only two bedrooms were planned. But once the project started, the owners were keen to add a third bedroom, mainly for guests. The architects conceived of a third circular-shaped room, about the same scale as the enclosed spiral staircase. The feeling is like being in a protected shade house, with views of the bushland below and on the deck, the experience of being among the trees.

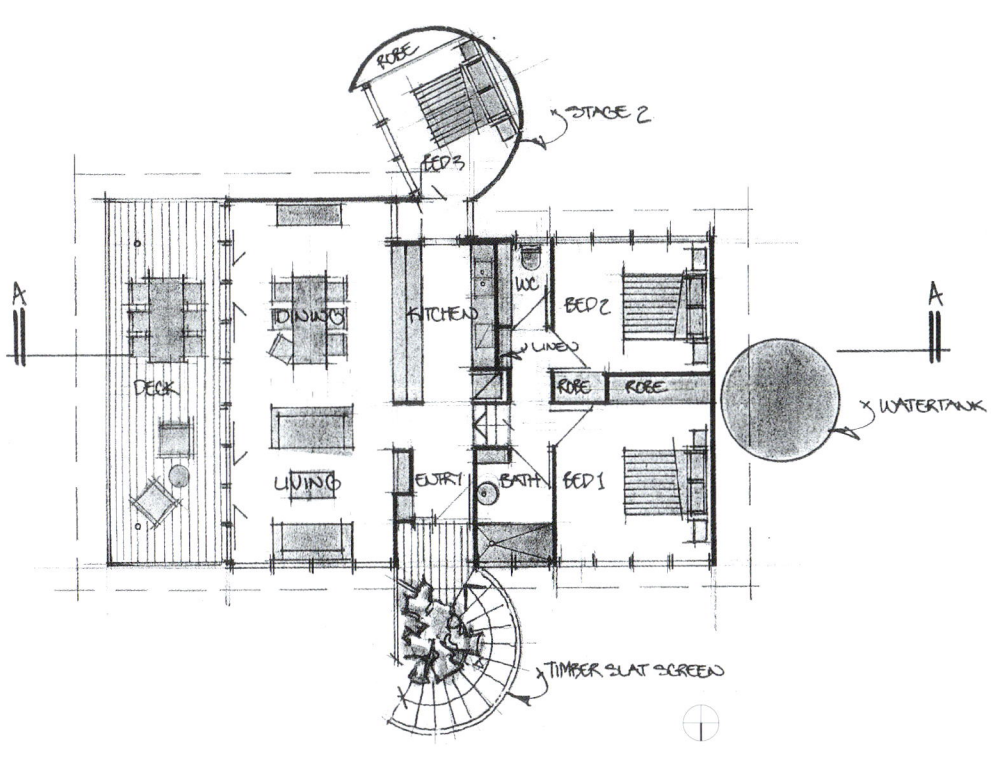

A Panoramic View

SJB ARCHITECTS AND SJB INTERIORS

Photography by Tony Miller

Few beach houses enjoy such a privileged position. A mere 25 metres from the water, this house overlooks grassy sand dunes.

Designed by SJB Architects and SJB Interiors, the new house is one of a handful along the water's edge. Replacing an old beach shack with a new house gave the architects an opportunity to match the design with the location. The focus is on the beach, the bay and the sand dunes.

The owners, who have grown-up children, not only wanted a design commensurate with the view, but also a house that could be used when the children weren't there. "They didn't want to be greeted with a series of large rooms that weren't going to be occupied," says architect Alfred de Bruyne. So the architects created two living zones that could be occupied independently of each other.

On the top floor are the main bedroom, ensuite, kitchen and living area. On the ground floor are three bedrooms, main kitchen and living area. Both levels have generous access to the outdoor areas. On the ground level, the walls of the house are extended to frame the outdoor areas, creating privacy and protection from the wind. And on the second level, there is a continuous outdoor deck that wraps around the entire space. While the outdoor space, framed with glass balconies, appears exposed to the elements, a retractable awning on the roof can be used for protection. "It's automated. You can quickly batten down when the weather changes," says de Bruyne.

The façade is clad in western red cedar. Crisp and contemporary, it presents a modest face to the street. However, once through the front door, full-length glass windows face the view. As de Bruyne says, "The design celebrates the position. It's a regular-sized block, but you don't feel as if you are hemmed in. The neighbour's front gardens are part of the larger picture. You could be simply anywhere."

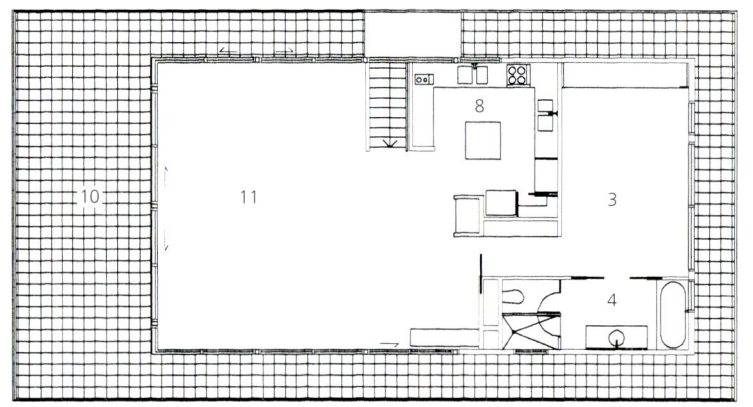

1 Verandah
2 Entry
3 Bedroom
4 Ensuite
5 Bathroom
6 Laundry
7 Store
8 Kitchen
9 Recreation room
10 Terrace
11 Living/dining

43

Nestled into the Bush
BRUCE RICKARD & ASSOCIATES
Photography by Eric Sierens of Max Dupain & Associates

This beach house, on the edge of a pebbled and sandy strip, is the work of architect Bruce Rickard. Nestled into its bushland setting, the form of the house is difficult to make out. Much better defined is the view of the water from the main living areas on the upper floor.

The orientation to the light and the water correspond, so each room enjoys the warmth and 'ripple' of the bay. The living area takes up the entire top floor and the bedrooms occupy the lower floor. Designed for a single person, who has numerous friends all around the country, the brief included a generous open-plan living area for entertaining. The large terrace, extending from the living area, is framed with a steel pergola. "Originally the idea was to include a moveable canvas awning that could be folded and packed away. But my client prefers to use an old sail when the sun becomes too strong," says architect Bruce Rickard.

On the edge of the living area, hovering between the inside and the outside of the house, Rickard designed a series of concrete benches. "They take on a different function depending on whether the doors are left open or closed. They can function as either a seat or a table. There's no strict division. People can relax either indoors or outside on the decks," says Rickard, who also used exposed aggregate for the columns supporting the house. "I didn't want to design a massive building in this bushland. I wanted to keep it relatively lightweight to minimise the disturbance of the site," says Rickard.

Large Oregon trusses with posts not only create a decorative element within the house, but also define the open-plan spaces, giving some definition to the kitchen and living areas. The new house is clearly more than a beach shack. But hidden in the bush it's the view of the water rather than the house that makes the greatest statement.

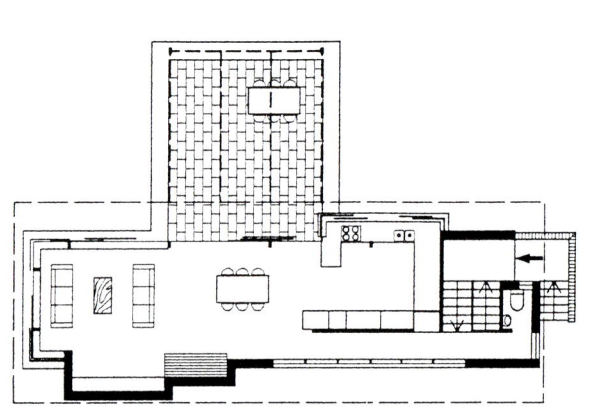

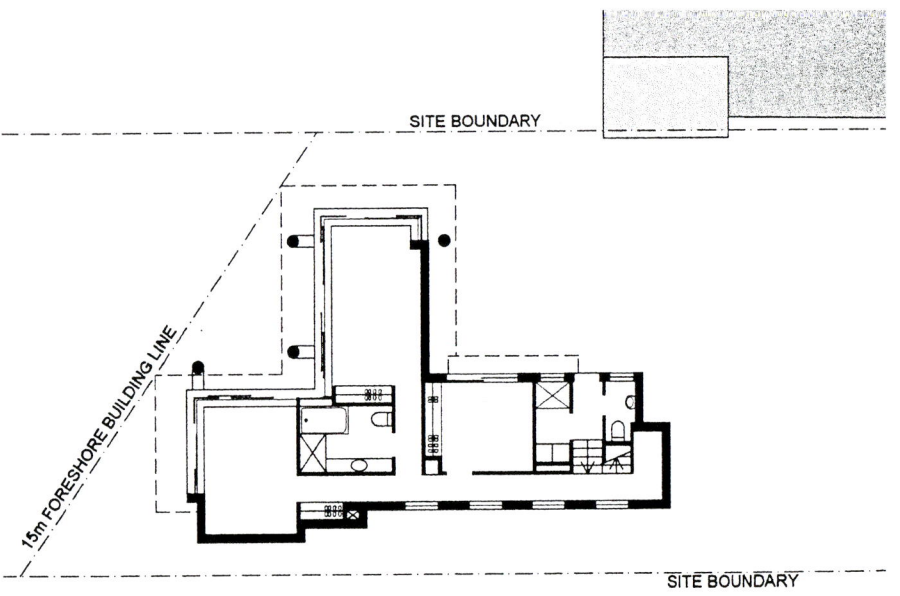

SITE BOUNDARY

15m FORESHORE BUILDING LINE

SITE BOUNDARY

0 1 2   4m

A Contrast of Styles

LACOSTE + STEVENSON ARCHITECTS

Photography by Brett Boardman

This timber beach house, originally built in the 1930s, remained unaltered for many years. The owners, who bought the home in the 1970s, went to live overseas for a while. However, after 25 years, they returned, and while the surrounds of their beach house had remained idyllic, the house appeared considerably less so. "They were attached to the house and the area, but they knew it required work," says architect Thierry Lacoste, who redesigned the house with his co-partner David Stevenson.

Located between a river and a national park, and surrounded by only a dozen houses, it's easy to understand the attraction of this area. However, with a house just 50 square metres in size, only the immediate family could enjoy what the area had to offer. The home consisted of two bedrooms and a fairly basic kitchen. "Our clients wanted their extended family to be able to stay over at the one time. The roster system wasn't working for them," says Lacoste.

Rather than design a completely new house, the architects extended the 50 square metres and almost tripled its size to 130 square metres. The existing kitchen was relocated to a more centralised position (occupying one of the bedrooms). And the enclosed verandah, which included the bathroom, was demolished. Two new wings were added. Facing the river, Lacoste and Stevenson designed one large living/dining space. With timber louvres at either end, this new space can be completely enclosed from or opened to the elements. Glass sliding doors can be pulled right back. "There's a large timber truss supporting the 12-metre expanse. It meant the living area could be free of columns, which would have detracted from the view," says Lacoste.

The architects could have tried to blend the old with the new. But in this case, they were keen to contrast the new work. The original timber was painted in blue, while the new timber was left in its natural state. The new extension, which is light and open, is also a contrast to the original rooms in the house, now used as bedrooms. Lined with ironbark and featuring high ceilings, these central rooms are relatively cool and dark. "They're great for bedrooms and are particularly appreciated during the warmer months," says Lacoste.

While the owners still manage to find time to travel, the space between visits to their beach house can be counted in weeks rather than years.

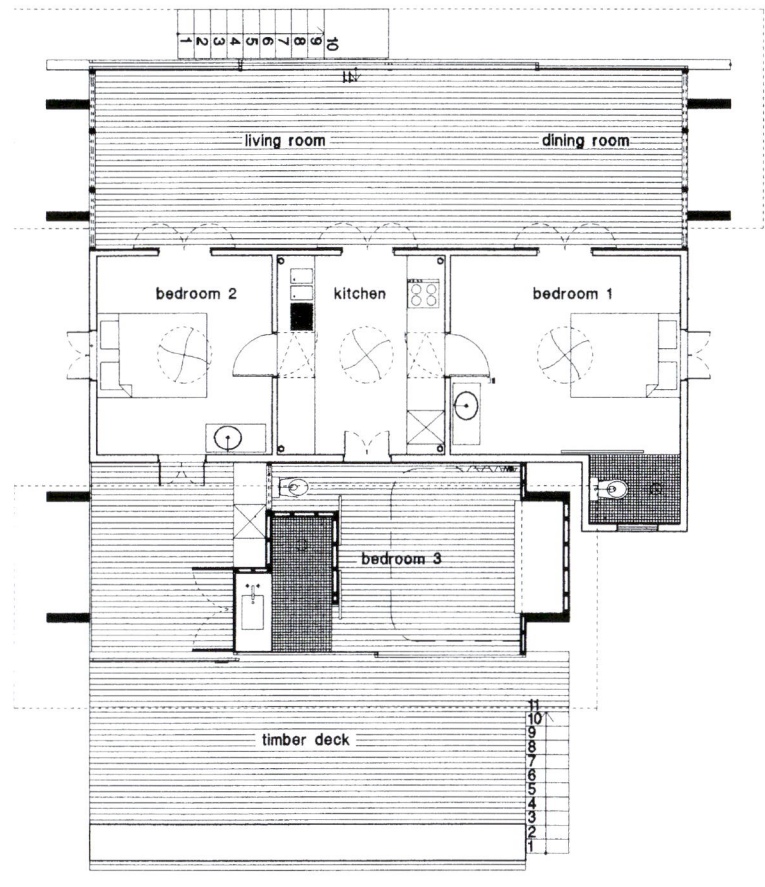

A Landmark

CON BASTIRAS ARCHITECT
Photography by Trevor Fox

Directly opposite a popular beach, this house is a landmark in the area. Designed by architect Con Bastiras, this large home (approximately 500 square metres), made of glass, steel and masonry, enjoys 180-degree views.

To create privacy, Bastiras designed a 1.8-metre-high sandstone fence. Passers-by need to strain their necks to look into the front yard. "The stone acts as a plinth for the house. We used the same stone that was used to protect the beachfront," says Bastiras.

While there is a view towards the beach, there is also a more private view onto the lap pool on the site. The L-shaped house (to accommodate the pool) maximises its street frontage. "Every room has a view of the beach. The view was an important component of the brief." Another feature is a prominent fireplace, which temporarily distracts the owners during the colder months of the year. Set in soaring glass windows (many of which double in height), the fireplace is clearly expressed in the home's exterior. "It's a modernist symbolic form," says Bastiras. To control the light and heat entering the house, the architect manipulated the amount of glass used. To create protection from the harsher sunlight, one upper-level wall is entirely finished with masonry.

The main kitchen and living areas open directly onto the lap pool. Voids allow both the light and views to enter the home from numerous angles. "I wanted to create a sculptural form with this house. It's more like an object in space," says Bastiras, who was keen to play with volume. The kitchen, for example, was deliberately pared back so that the surrounds could be fully appreciated. And rather than focusing on materials, Bastiras emphasised the structural forms with the house. The main staircase, for example, was designed to express the underside rather than the balustrades. "The underlying form creates intriguing shadows on the wall. It's quite sculptural," he says.

1 Entry
2 Dining
3 Living
4 Laundry
5 Store
6 Kitchen
7 Bathroom
8 Meals
9 Entertaining
10 Family
11 Drying court
12 Study
13 Bedroom
14 Robe
15 Ensuite
16 Balcony
17 Void
18 Garage
19 Stair to cellar
20 Lap pool

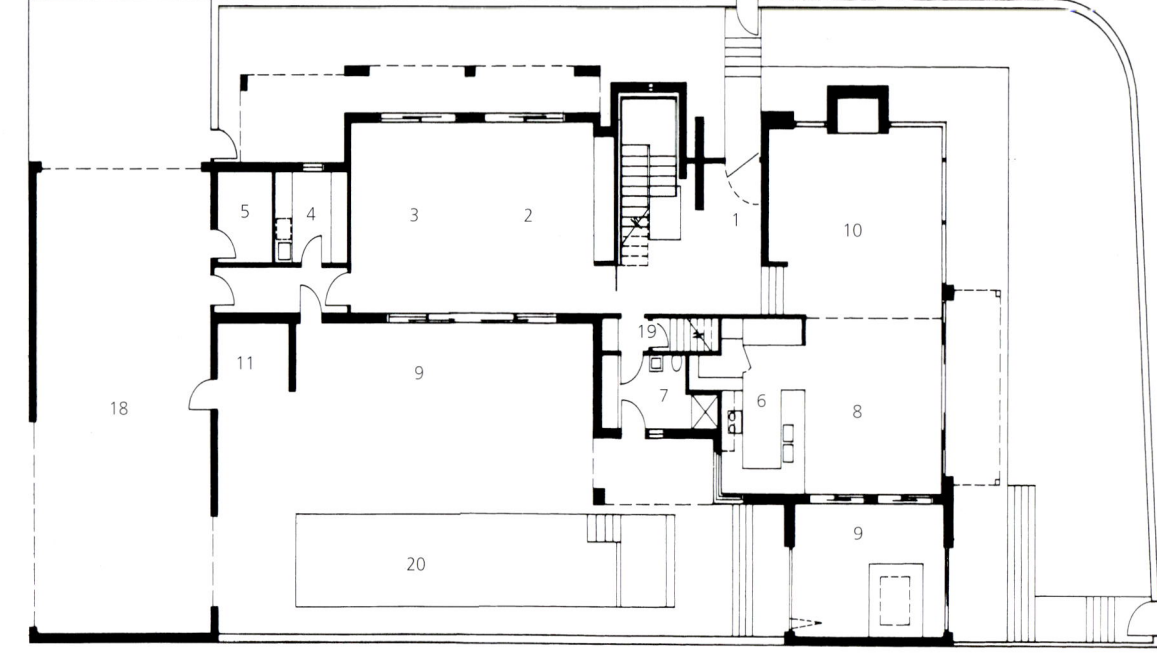

53

One Form

ODDEN RODRIGUES ARCHITECTS
Photography by Robert Frith

This large coastal reserve, covered with heath, was once an important transport link for goods. "There's still the remains of old marshalling yards," says architect Simon Rodrigues of Odden Rodrigues Architects, who designed this house for his family.

Originally consisting of two small sites, one 250 square metres, the other 275 square metres, a rudimentary shack built in the 1950s was the only structure on the site. Located only 20 minutes from the centre of town, the coastal site in a premier beach suburb necessitated the development of two houses. "The land was expensive, but I didn't want the two houses to appear as two separate buildings. I wanted the design to read as one house and appear to be wrapped in the one form," says Rodrigues.

The two houses both share a similar floor plan and scale. Both houses are designed over three levels, with 90 square metres on each floor. The basement level, which provides for car parking, is also used for the children's play area. The first floor includes the kitchen, dining and living areas and the third level of the house accommodates the three bedrooms.

Rodrigues was keen to create a sense of space in the main living areas. One of the few intrusions into the space is a concrete column, which acts as a structural support. Even the division between the kitchen and the living area was reduced to the bare minimum, with only structural steel beams supporting the glass shelves in the kitchen. "I wanted the house to feel like a simple container." The materials for the house were deliberately restrained. The brickwork is rendered and a corrugated zincalum roof has been extended to form the finish on one entire wall. Only a few windows punctuate the façade.

"The summers can be extremely hot. I didn't want to have to rely on airconditioning to make the house pleasurable to live in," says Rodrigues. Instead of large glass sliding doors to the patios, the architect chose Alaskan yellow cedar. "I wanted the materials and finishes to respond to the environment. I've used off-whites, greys and straw yellow for the doors. The doors fit into the colouration of the sand dunes," he says.

1 Living
2 Kitchen
3 Bathroom
4 Bedroom
5 Courtyard
6 Balcony

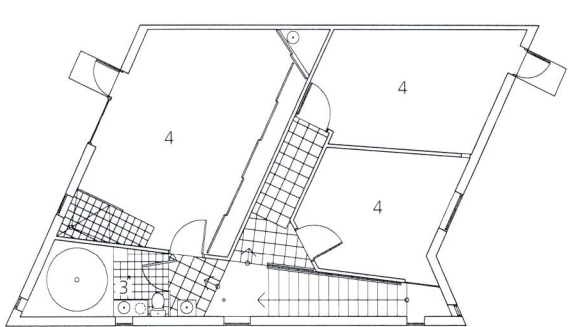

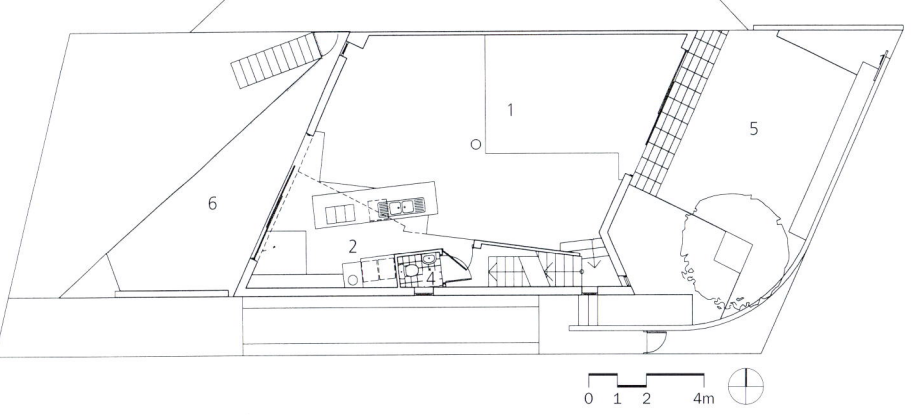

0 1 2   4m

A Series of Boxes

BBP ARCHITECTS

Photography by Chris Ott

An elevated site, overlooking a bay, required a beach-house design that would take in the panoramic views. Designed by BBP Architects, this three-tiered house includes a garage on the ground level, two bedrooms on the first level, a kitchen/living/dining area on the third level and two bedrooms and a bathroom above. While the ceiling heights are generous on each level, the architects were required to not exceed the height limit of 7 metres above ground level. "It set up the envelope to work from," says architect David Balestra-Pimpini of BBP Architects.

The architects were keen to ensure all the living spaces had views. Apart from the service areas (such as the laundry and bathrooms), all the bedrooms and living spaces have an unimpeded view of the water. "We were loosely inspired by the aesthetics of a 1950s pole-framed beach house. This residence acknowledges simple relaxed retreat-like qualities, without being retrospective," says Balestra-Pimpini. Glass, steel, metal cladding and stone create a new language for this weekend retreat.

The house, which is approximately 350 square metres, was designed in a series of square boxes, supported by a light steel structure. Like the exterior, which features elements such as glass balustrades, the interior spaces feature open timber staircases with wire stainless-steel cabling that allows the spaces to appear continuous rather than segmented. Creating a double void over the living/dining area, also accentuates the transparency within the home. Large glass sliding doors to the balconies further blur the division between indoor and outdoor areas.

As Balestra-Pimpini says, "The owners simply provided a list of the rooms that were required, four bedrooms, two bathrooms and a need to engage with the view. Keeping it simple is our mantra."

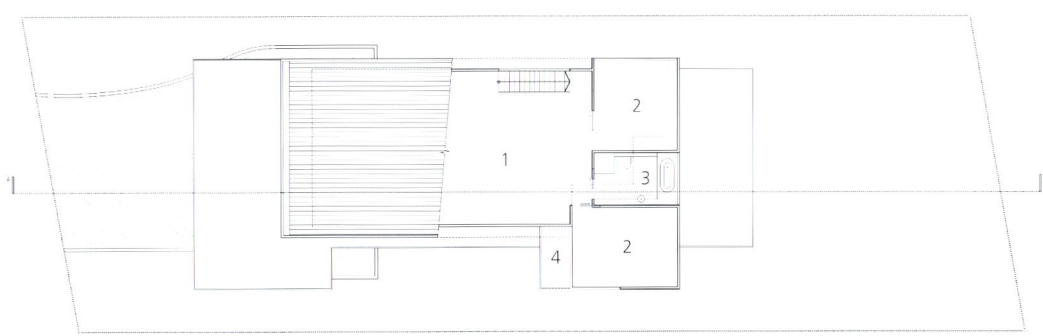

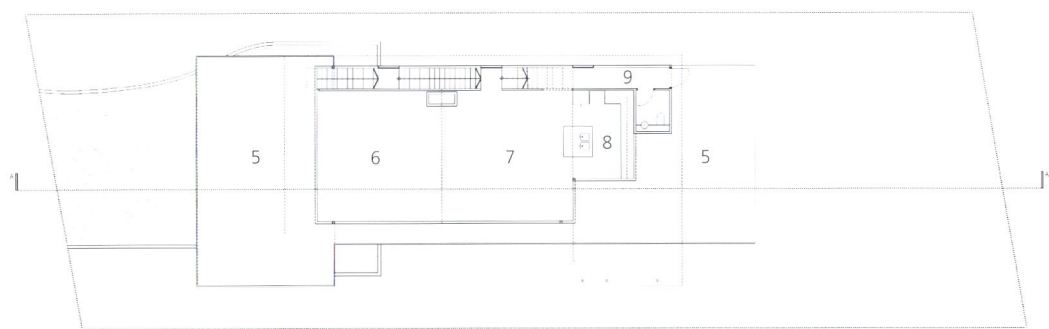

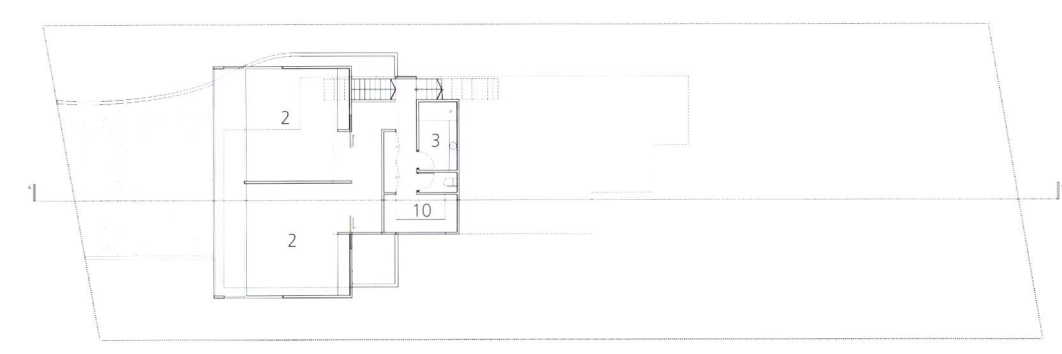

1 Dining below
2 Bedroom
3 Bathroom
4 Balcony
5 Deck
6 Living
7 Dining
8 Kitchen
9 Passage
10 Laundry

A Sense of Scale

DAWSON BROWN ARCHITECTURE

Photography by Robert Brown

Located on a heavily forested site, the original house must have been one of the first to be built (circa 1910) in the area. Keen to retain the board- and batten-wall cottage, but requiring significantly more accommodation, the clients requested a separate freestanding building, one that would compliment the existing house.

Situated on a cliff face, with a 10-metre fall to the ocean, architects Dawson Brown were keen to create a distinction between the new building and the period home. However, to unify the composition, the architects used the same materials for the new studio wing – board and batten timber. The new two-storey tower (approximately 20 square metres in size), is accessed from a bridge and separated from the cottage by the swimming pool. "We wanted to keep the scale of the original house and keep it quite distinct from the studio. The tower (which includes a bedroom and bathroom on the lower level and a studio above) is more like a piece of sculpture in the bush rather than an addition to the house," says architect Robert Brown.

To anchor the studio into its bushland setting, the architects braced the house with recycled ironbark. The oversized crossbeams create decorative as well as structural support to the house. "They were inspired by the old deckchairs which you would have sat on as a child," says Brown. "The elevation also allows plants to grow below," he adds.

The original cottage was extensively reworked too. The living area on the ground level was opened up entirely, with access to the wrap-around terraces. And below, two new bedrooms were designed, both with ensuite bathrooms. One bathroom includes a porthole window looking into the swimming pool.

While the new studio provides a contemporary edge to the complex, there is still a connection to the past. The woven timber balustrades enclosing the studio verandah are imbued with a sense of craft, inspired by the Arts and Crafts period at the turn of the last century. "We didn't want to create one large house. We wanted to keep the scale of both buildings and a sense of the original craft."

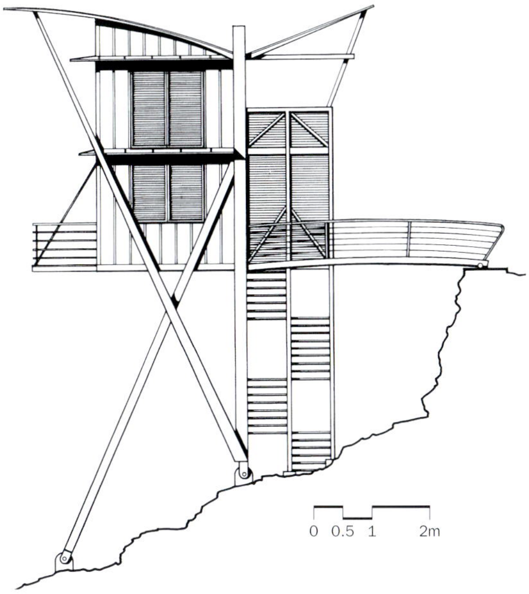

1 Entry
2 Dining
3 Terrace
4 Kitchen
5 Store
6 W.C.
7 Living
8 Pool
9 Bridge
10 Bedroom
11 Balcony
12 Bathroom
13 Studio

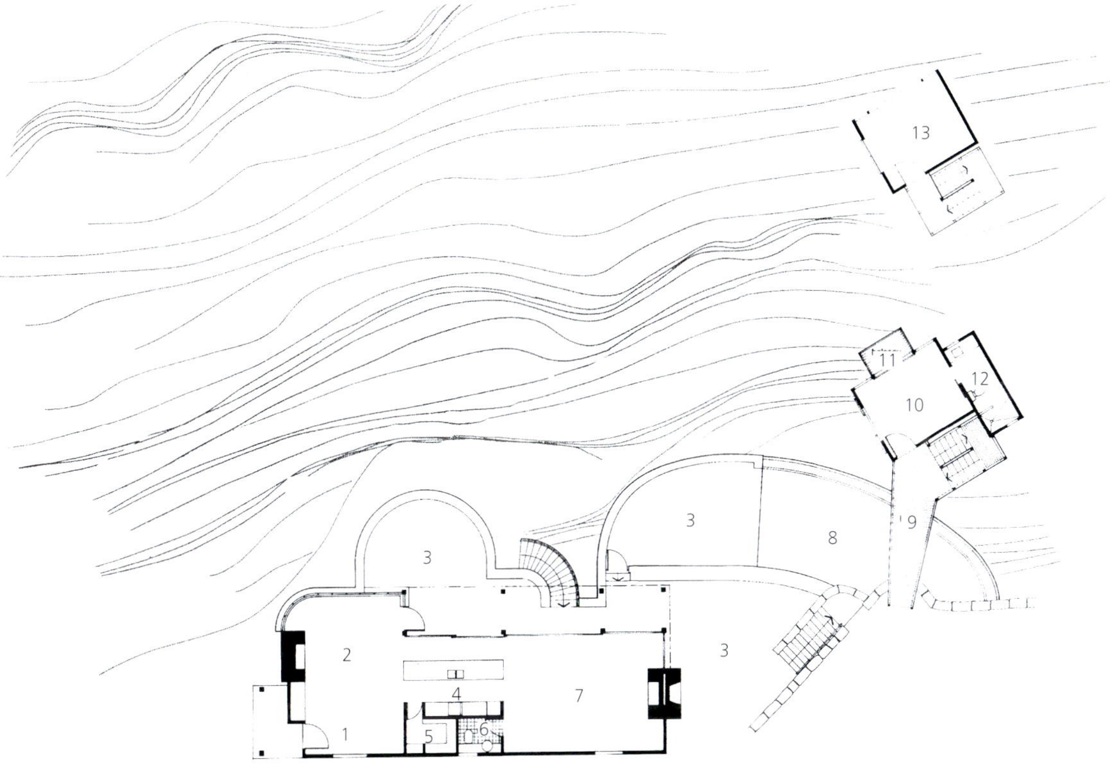

An Impressive Swathe

STEPHEN VARADY ARCHITECTURE

Photography by Stephen Varady

This new house on the coast cuts an impressive swathe through its natural bushland. With the sea in the distance and framed by established gum trees, the design is anchored into the landscape by solid blade walls, acting as the home's structural support and carefully framing each view.

"The design is an abstraction of the Miesian plan, with the rooms opening off a notional corridor along the northern edge. In response to the orientation and the slope of the site, I raised the living spaces into the canopy of the tress with the ancillary spaces below," says architect Stephen Varady who designed the house. Varady has deliberately manipulated the volumes to maximise the views. The major living, dining and kitchen areas are the highest spaces, flowing into each other and to the deck areas. The lower level comprises the children's rumpus room together with garaging facilities. While there is a continuous flow of different spaces, the bedrooms were conceived as self-contained spaces, with their own private balconies and unique outlook. Generous outdoor decks accompany each living area to ensure that the outdoors is integral to the design. The built-in outdoor spa bath allows for the sound of water, even when the sound of the nearby surf is muffled.

Mindful of variations in the coastal climate, Varady designed two deck areas, one facing towards the sun and the other protected from the harsh summer rays. The outdoor spaces can therefore be appreciated throughout the entire year. While dramatic blades direct the views, the wonderful native vegetation can also be appreciated in the more intimate spaces. The bark from the eucalyptus trees, for example, can almost be touched from inside the bathroom and ensuite areas of the house. "The guest bathrooms allow the visitors to feel like they're bathing in the trees," says Varady. Another option is to stroll to the nearby beach for the real experience.

Named 'Tea Gardens' (after its location), the image conjured up is of translucent walls set in an oriental garden. While not placed in an oriental garden, the house displays a similar sensitivity to its own unique coastal environment.

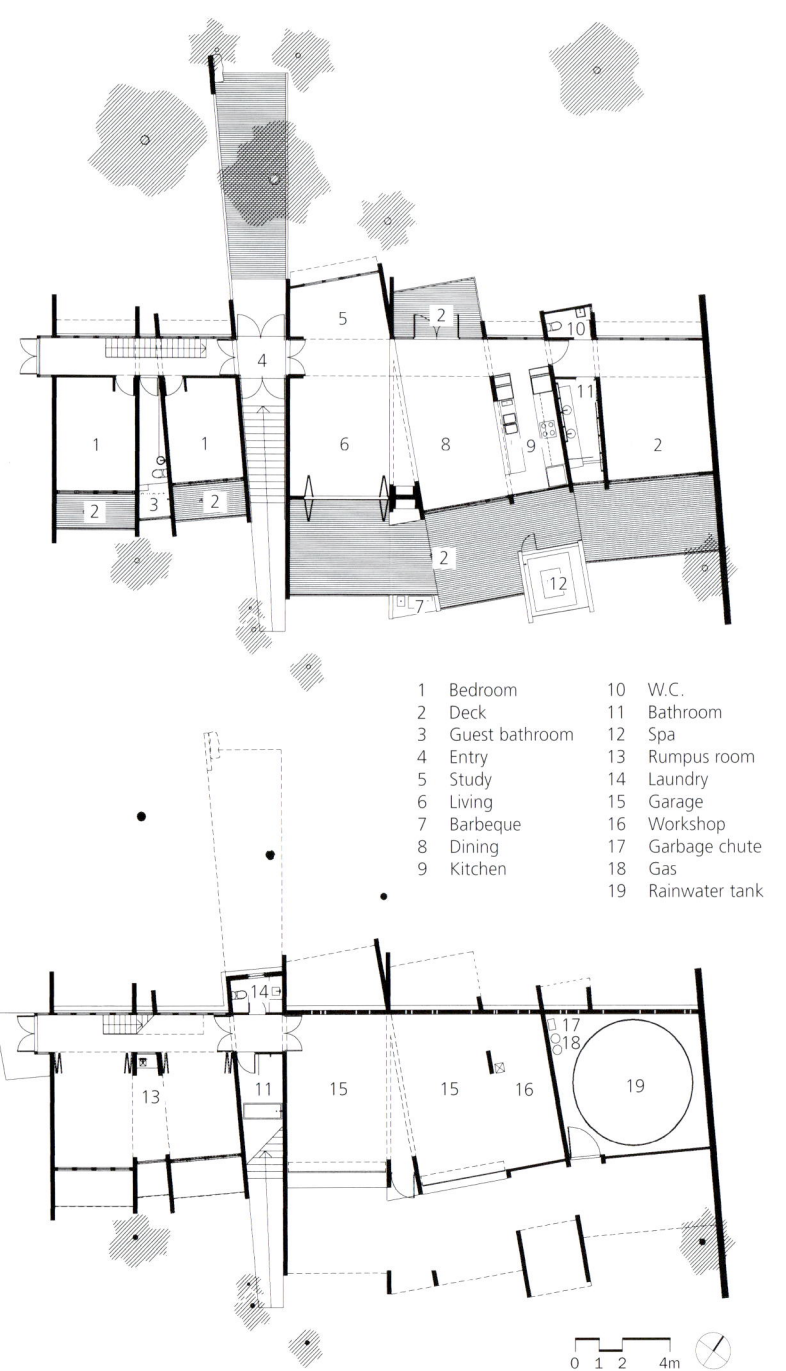

1	Bedroom	10	W.C.
2	Deck	11	Bathroom
3	Guest bathroom	12	Spa
4	Entry	13	Rumpus room
5	Study	14	Laundry
6	Living	15	Garage
7	Barbeque	16	Workshop
8	Dining	17	Garbage chute
9	Kitchen	18	Gas
		19	Rainwater tank

Casuarina Beach House

LAHZ NIMMO ARCHITECTS

Photography by Brett Boardman

This striking house, on Casuarina Beach, was designed with quite a simple strategy in mind – an open, breezily relaxed and extroverted 'living pavilion' juxtaposed with a two-storey shuttered timber 'sleeping box'. The two ideas were then linked by a double-height breezeway space, acting as both the entry and sheltered deck area of the house.

Designed by Lahz Nimmo Architects, the Casuarina Beach house is a landmark of the relatively flat topography. While the house currently sits within a large open site, it has been designed with future subdivision in mind. It responds to a relatively long narrow allotment, keeping in mind future homes. "The opposing stimuli of a piece of driftwood sitting in the sand and a floating jetty were starting points for this beach-house design. For the Casuarina Beach house, we used a combination of these two metaphors – anchoring the 'sleeping box' component on the site, while allowing the 'living pavilion' to be a hovering entity over the landscape," says architect Annabel Lahz.

The 'sleeping box' has a series of shutters and timber louvres which allow it to be opened or closed, depending on the owner's daylight requirements. The main living area was designed as a 'floating pavilion' in the landscape, sitting 900 millimetres above the ground plane. The elevation allows the occupants to view above the primary dune through to the beach and ocean. The 'living pavilion' includes the kitchen, dining and living areas, which are extended by a generous deck area. The 'sleeping box', as its name suggests, includes a garage and bedroom on the ground floor, with three bedrooms on the first floor. "The house was designed as a series of spaces that can be inhabited in different ways. The spaces experience different aspects of the site depending on the time of day, time of year or predominant breezes. Some spaces are not clearly defined as either internal or external. Some focus outwards towards the beach, others focus inwards toward the activities of the house," says Lahz.

As the house is relatively open to the elements, the architects included a breezeway. The protected verandah, which also doubles as the entry point to the house, provides protection from some of the prevailing coastal winds. The drying effect of the sun and the wind, combined with the salt air, creates a tough environment. In deference to these conditions, the architects used recycled and oiled hardwood, which will gradually fade in time.

Two Sides

DONALDSON + WARN ARCHITECTS
Photography by Martin Farquarson

This house has two distinct sides – one side faces the ocean, the other is a relatively suburban street. The only barrier between the ocean and the house is a small local park. Approaching the house from the street (the point of entry), the ocean could be miles away. "The slope of the site is 3 metres. It makes the beach appear even more distant (although the surf can be heard)," says architect Dick Donaldson of Donaldson + Warn Architects, who designed this beach house.

The wedge-shaped site, which has an 8-metre frontage to the beach, fans out towards the street behind. Though the beachside is fairly narrow, the owners wanted views from all windows. "The solution was to bring the circulation zone in contact with the views, as well as into the main living areas," says Donaldson.

On the ground level, facing the street is the garage, storage areas, a wine cellar and an office. The first level includes living, dining and a casual living area together with bedrooms for two children. There's also a separate play area for the children. On the top level, there's the main bedroom and parent's retreat. The view to the ocean can be appreciated from the first floor and on the top level, well above the dunes, a large folding door can be pulled right back to reveal the ocean. The bedroom and the retreat then become the one room.

The two sides of the house (one to the ocean and one to the street), have been treated quite differently by the architects, particularly in the materials used. To the street, the architects used solid masonry wall, while on the beachside, there is a considerably lighter treatment, with the emphasis on glass, timber, aluminium and steel. "It's deliberately lighter towards the beach. It was an appropriate response," says Donaldson.

The sound of the ocean draws in those visiting the area, and for the fortunate owners, the ocean views can be appreciated immediately past the front door.

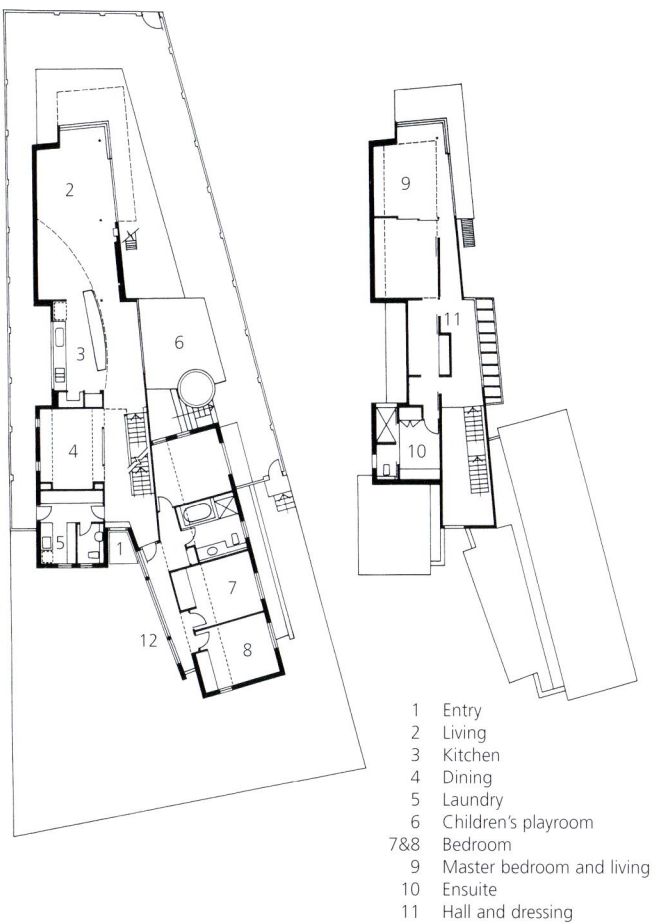

1 Entry
2 Living
3 Kitchen
4 Dining
5 Laundry
6 Children's playroom
7&8 Bedroom
9 Master bedroom and living
10 Ensuite
11 Hall and dressing
12 Garage below

The Original Footprint

SAM CRAWFORD ARCHITECT

Photography by Brett Boardman

This house evokes the memory of a 1950s beach shack. This isn't surprising, given that the footprint of the original home was retained, complete with a definitive 1950s-style skillion roof. Designed by Sam Crawford and Emili Fox, while finishing their architectural studies at university, the house is now a completely new beach house. "Nearly everything was replaced – windows, doors and even the original shiplap weatherboards. They were completely rotten," says Crawford, who was advised by many builders, at the time, to demolish the home completely and start again.

As the owners had fond memories of growing up in the house as children, they were keen to retain as much of the original structure as possible. The external wall structure, the floor joists, the rafters and the roof sheeting were retained. And one bedroom remains in its original position. Everything else has been added and reconfigured. Vertical tongue-and-groove weatherboard replaced the shiplap boards and while the original roof was retained, new glass highlight windows create a more transparent feel to the home. "We wanted to take advantage of the vertical elements of the gum trees and bring more light into the living areas," says Crawford.

The interior was substantially redesigned. The kitchen and main bathroom were swapped around. A bedroom, once enclosed, was opened up and now forms part of the dining/living area. Large timber and glass sliding doors were also installed either side of the house, framing both the casual meals area and the living spaces. "When you open the doors onto the front deck and to the rear (adjacent to the kitchen/meals area), the spaces feel considerably larger than the home's 120 square metres," says Crawford. One of the few additions, apart from the new deck areas, is the main bedroom and ensuite. Following the gentle topography of the site, the main bedroom is reached via a few steps. "It adds a certain privacy to the otherwise open-plan house."

With the opening up of the house, the ventilation is also significantly improved. "Before, while one whole façade was wall-to-ceiling glass, filling the place with sun and light, the other remained entirely closed. During warmer months, it felt like you were living in a green house," says Crawford.

Straightforward and unpretentious, this beach house still has the feel of an original 1950s weekender. The fifties laminates have been replaced and the new kitchen allows for more sophisticated dining. However, for the owners, there is still the rudimentary feel of simply living near the beach.

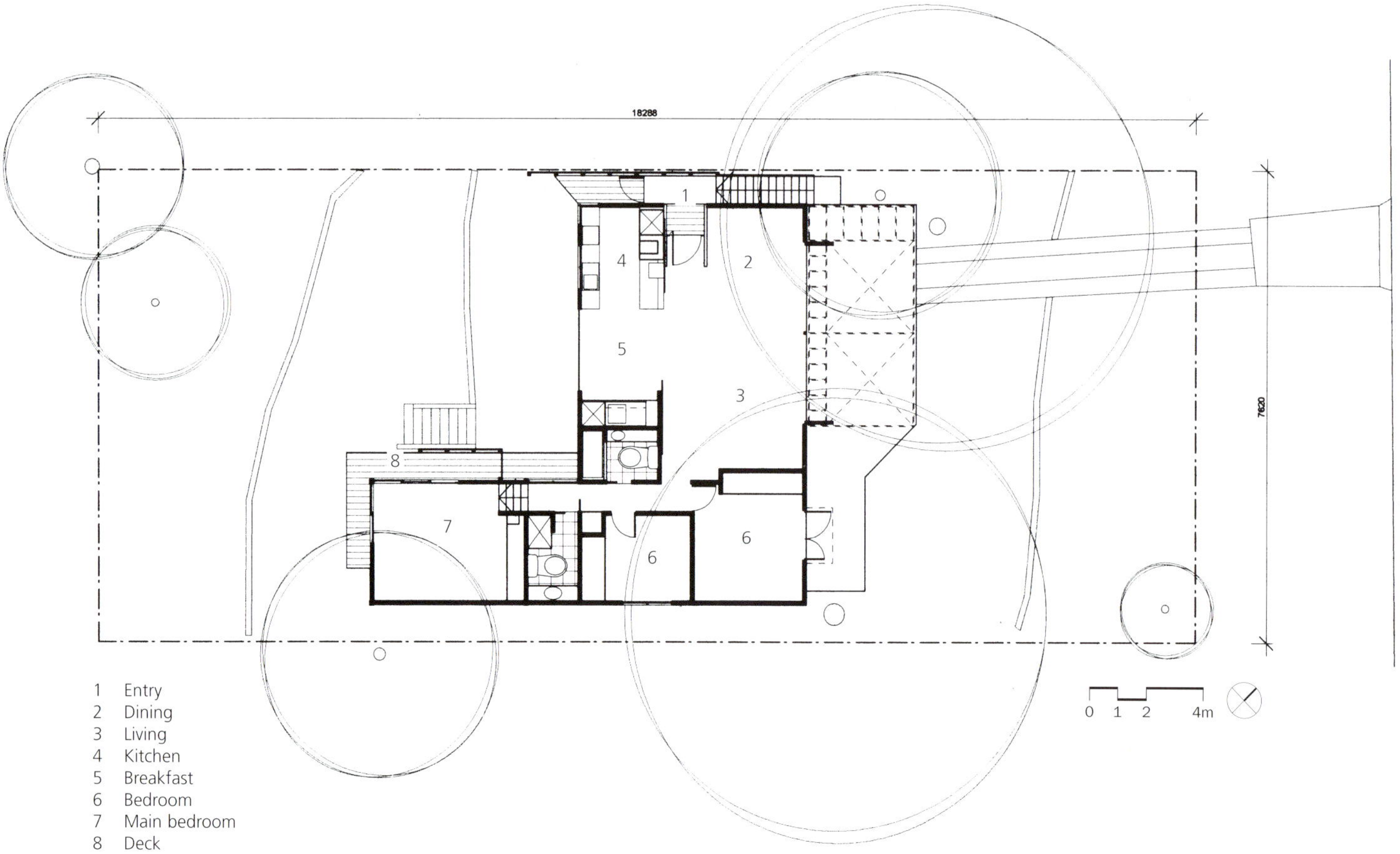

1 Entry
2 Dining
3 Living
4 Kitchen
5 Breakfast
6 Bedroom
7 Main bedroom
8 Deck

Anchored to the Landscape

EDMISTON JONES ARCHITECTS

Photography by Peter Rae

This beach house, designed by Edmiston Jones Architects, is located on a gently sloping site. Overlooking a man-made dam and gully, rather than the ocean, it's a quiet rural oasis. "The design of the house allows it to 'spread' into the landscape, by following the contours of the land," says architect Brandt Noack of Edmiston Jones Architects.

The owners, a retired diplomat and an academic, wanted a relatively neutral canvas, where they could store their hundreds of books and artefacts collected from all parts of the globe. The house was designed in three pavilions. The first, upon entering the house, includes two bedrooms. The second pavilion includes the main living area, kitchen and dining area. Two large outdoor decks flank either side of this pavilion, one leads from the dining area, the other from the lounge. The third pavilion consists of the main bedroom and ensuite. Unlike the two other pavilions, this one consists of a separate structure. Tilted to focus on views of the dam, it's like a raised platform in space. While the third pavilion is linked to the main living areas via a covered walkway, this has no walls. "It gives the owners the opportunity to come into direct contact with the elements every morning," says Noack.

The three pavilions are made in fairly lightweight materials. The structure is a lightweight steel portal frame, clad in timber and fibro-cement. And there's generous glazing from all angles. In contrast to these light materials, Edmiston Jones used a curved rendered wall to create a forecourt. "It's also an anchoring device for the lighter materials," says Noack, who likens the solid wall to the remnants of an old chimney, once the outer shell of the house has disintegrated. "It also creates a screen to the pavilions and privacy from the road."

The only element that can be seen beyond the curved wall is the angled steel roof. To focus on the established trees, the architects included several highlight windows in the design. Past the entrance, there's total seclusion.

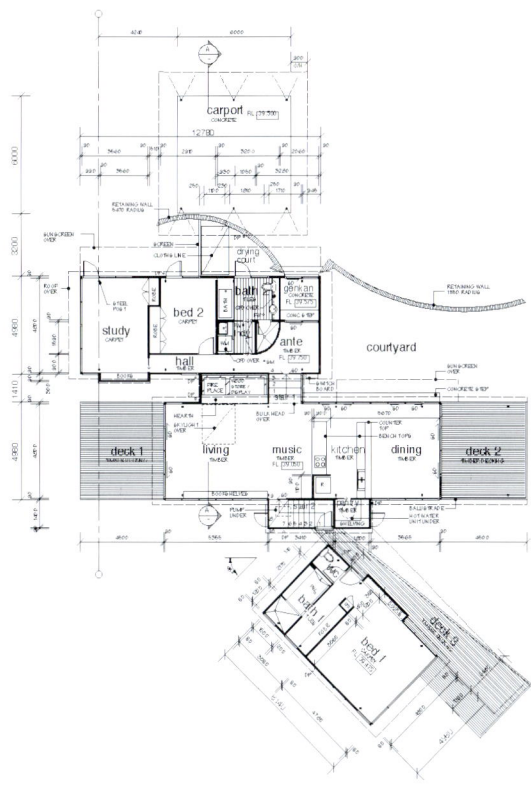

Above the Dunes
DESIGN KING COMPANY
Photography by Brett Boardman

Perched above a sand dune, this house was originally conceived on a lower 'rung' of the dune. Overlooking the beach and native bushland, the site has a 20-degree slope. "My client didn't think it was possible to build on top of the dune. It was only after we walked over the site together and took in the panoramic views that we decided to elevate the house to where we felt it belonged," says architect Jon King, who designed the house.

When the survey plans were released, both the architect and client realised building on top of the dune was a possibility. "The main issue was getting materials to the top including all the machinery that's required," says King. To achieve the best result, a lightweight structure was selected, a tubular steel frame and steel-studded walls. "A significant part of the house had to be prefabricated offsite. Many of the joints had to be welded prior to their delivery," he says. To anchor the house into the sensitive sand dune, up to 20 steel screw piles were buried well into the sand. "It was a substantial cost of the project. But my clients were willing to pull back in other areas to have the house up on the dune," he says.

The relatively compact house consists of two bedrooms, a study, a kitchen, an open living/dining area and generous outdoor deck areas, incised into the plan. One roof plane covers the entire house and generous glazed window-walls are punctuated with louvres. "The decks provide more sheltered areas. They also allow the views to be appreciated even from the bathrooms," says King.

There are no large architectural gestures in this house. Delight comes from its simplicity and the house's strong connection to its sensitive surrounds. However, while the clients were keen to reduce the detail, they weren't prepared to leave their grand piano out of the plans. "It was one of the few things that were clearly specified in the brief," says King. Its presence on the living room floor is a reminder of the strength of the home's construction, rather than the fragility of the sand dune below.

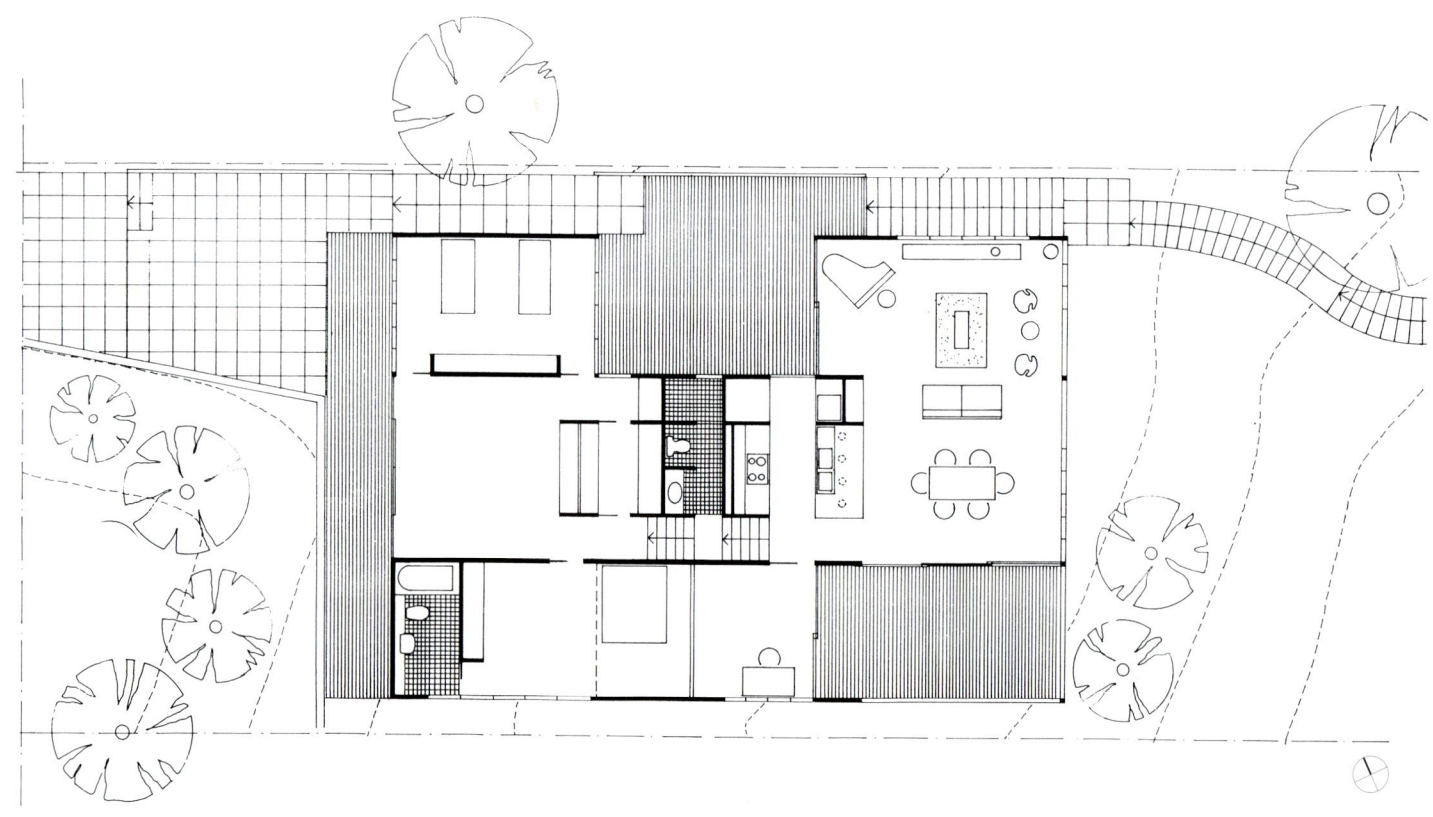

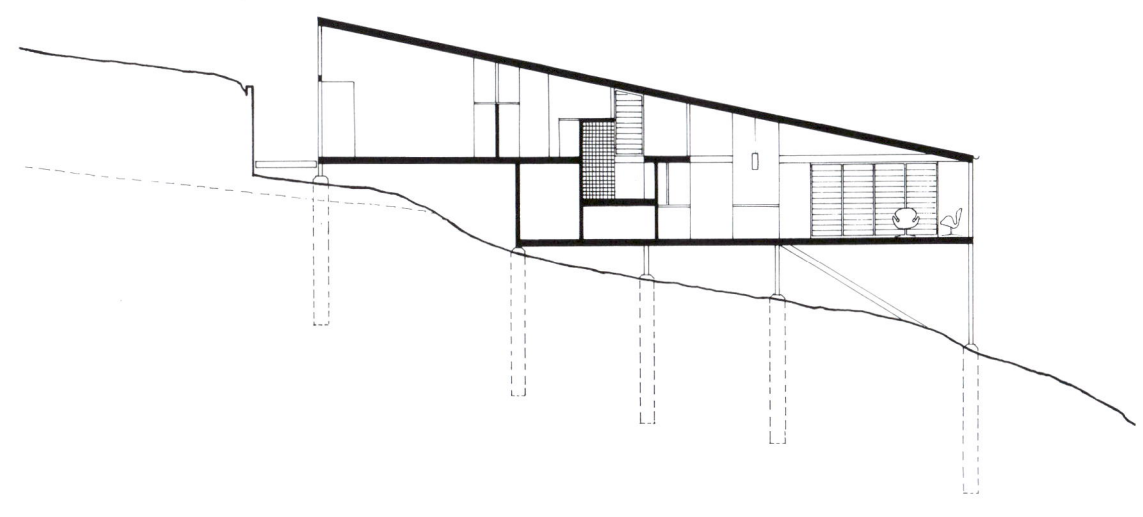

81

Sculptural Form

MARCUS O'REILLY ARCHITECT

Photography by Robert Ashton

Designed by architect Marcus O'Reilly, the owners of this home wanted more than a beach house. They were after something that could be used as a permanent residence down the track.

After renovating their city terrace, the owners gave O'Reilly a fairly open brief. "The only things they asked for were three bedrooms and one large living area," says O'Reilly. "They also mentioned they were keen to include a friend in the project, who specialised in rammed earth," he adds. Appreciative of the qualities of this technique, O'Reilly included rammed earth in his design. "It has a monumental feel, but it doesn't appear heavy. It has a wonderful tactile quality as well as being thermally responsive."

The other main material used for the house is galvanised steel, corrugated and flat. "It will eventually weather to a more muted grey, similar to the bushland," says O'Reilly, who also used local limestone to create a sculptural entrance to the house. The 400-millimetre rammed-earth wall, which acts as the main spine wall, dissects two lighter steel wing-like pavilions. "The rammed-earth wall anchors the house into the landscape and separates the living and sleeping areas (the parent's bedroom and study on the ground floor and the children's bedrooms and study above)," he says. The galvanised-steel aqueduct, expressed in the living room and outside the house, is both a functional and whimsical addition. The duct not only recycles the rainwater but it is also used as a frame to attach the children's play equipment. And in the living room, steel ladders are attached to the underside of the duct. "They double as ladders for the children to climb. Alternatively, they can be used to hang up beach towels to dry," says O'Reilly.

To maximise the views and sunlight, O'Reilly created a tiered design, with the largest windows appearing at ground level and narrowing above. "At night, there's quite a unique glow to the interior and during the day the light plays against the rammed-earth wall," says O'Reilly, who angled the ceiling height from 2.7 metres to 4 metres to maximise the sunlight.

To compliment the texture of the rammed earth, polished concrete floors were used in the living area. Materials such as cypress and jarrah were used for the kitchen joinery. "It was picking up the textures of the site. The soft and natural earthy colours of the site were instrumental in shaping the design," says O'Reilly.

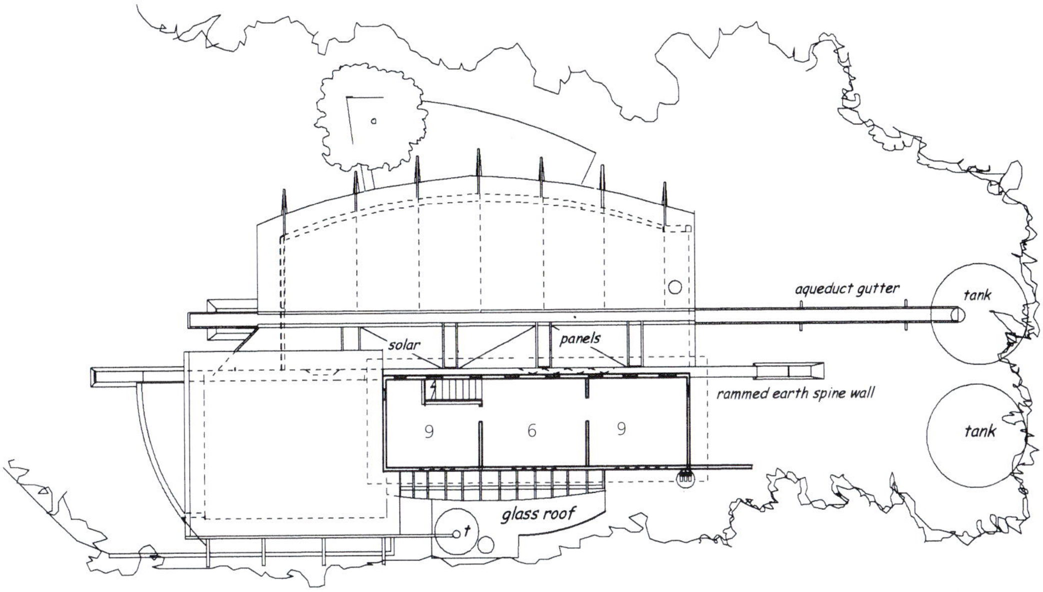

1 Dining
2 Lounge
3 Kitchen
4 Sitting
5 Patio
6 Study
7 Laundry
8 Bathroom
9 Bedroom
10 Balcony
11 Carport under
12 Covered porch

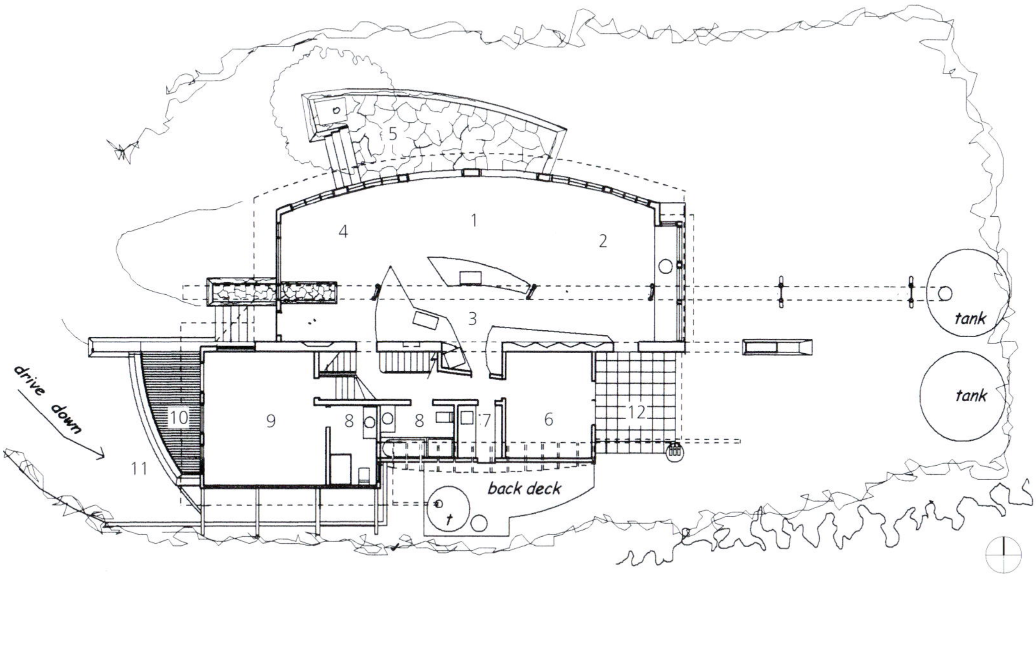

A Tropical Retreat

ELIZABETH WATSON BROWN ARCHITECTS

Photography by Eric Victor of Perdreux and by David Sandison

This house, spread over a hectare of tropical bushland, is the perfect retreat for a couple of city dwellers. In contrast to their city apartment, this house is gently cradled by the landscape.

Designed by architect Elizabeth Watson Brown, the 250-square-metre house is constructed of rendered concrete blocks, glass and timber. "I wanted to ensure sea views from every room and to make sure light could enter the house from every angle," says Watson Brown. To achieve these goals, the architect designed the house as four interlinked components. These include a main kitchen and living pavilion, a guest suite (with kitchen and bathroom), a separate library and a main bedroom. Instead of a central passage linking all these spaces, an internal/external walkway meanders between the enclosed areas and the garden areas. The walkway, made of concrete pavers embedded with river pebbles, is defined by large sliding glass window-walls. "They slide right back and you feel like you're walking in the garden. But you don't get wet when it rains (the walkways are covered)," says Watson Brown.

The clients, who had collected oriental textiles and artefacts over the years, were keen to create a Balinese feel in the home. Water was an important element and takes the form of a central pond and swimming pool. The terrace divides the watery surfaces. "The boundaries disappear. There's an ambiguity about the edge. The garden and its fragrances were important in the design. There's a sense of living in the garden, even when you're undercover," says Watson Brown. "In a sense, the house has been fragmented. Everything isn't under the one roof," she adds.

There are a few delineations in the house that are a reminder of the division between the indoors and outdoors. Slightly raised timber flooring in the living area is a subtle reminder that one is moving indoors. "But it also feels as though you are moving across a verandah," she says. Ventilation was also a key factor in the design. In a tropical climate, the rooms can enjoy the breezes. "The house cools down very quickly."

While the house is only 250 square metres, it feels considerably larger and more spacious. "I have borrowed from the garden. The site is quite rural and there are no neighbours nearby. It really allowed me to open up the house in all directions and make the most of what the site had to offer. I didn't want to create any secondary or lower-quality spaces without light, views and aspect," she says.

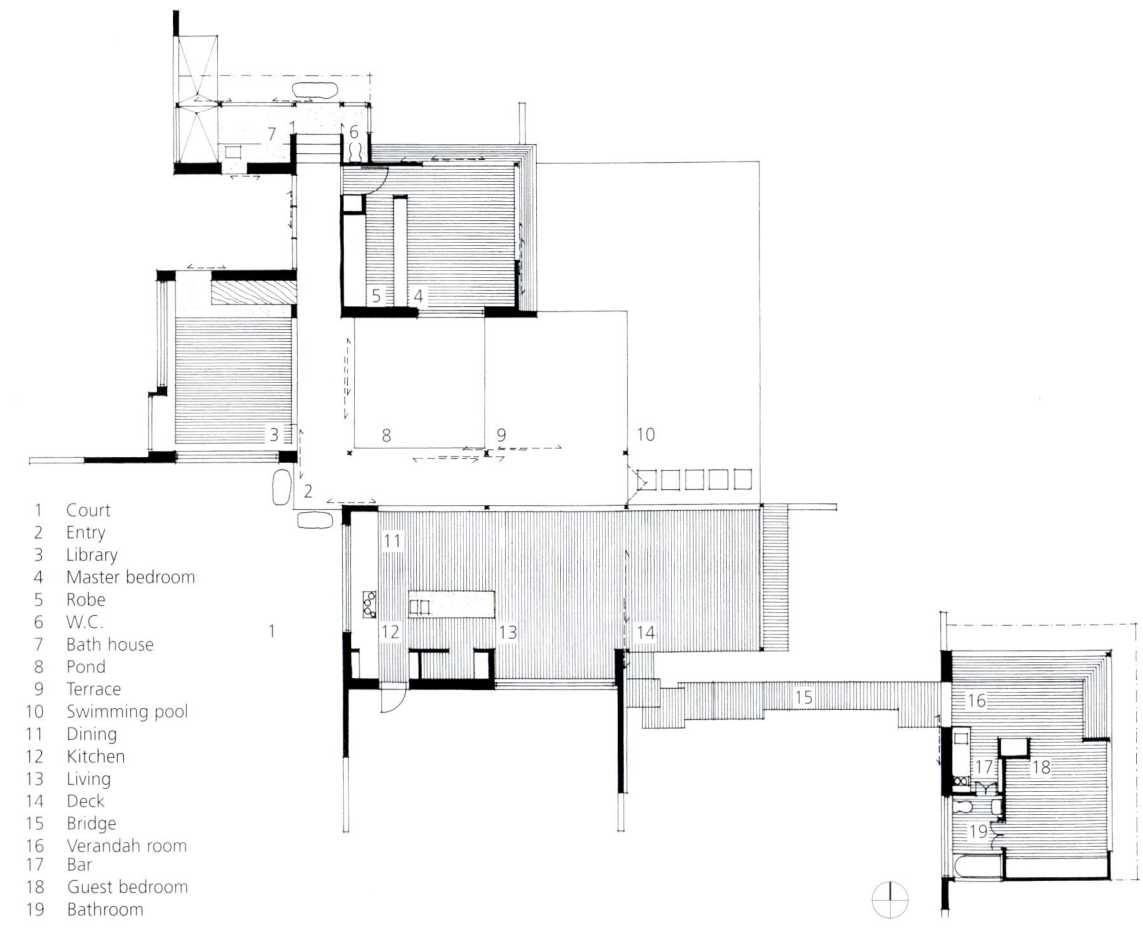

1 Court
2 Entry
3 Library
4 Master bedroom
5 Robe
6 W.C.
7 Bath house
8 Pond
9 Terrace
10 Swimming pool
11 Dining
12 Kitchen
13 Living
14 Deck
15 Bridge
16 Verandah room
17 Bar
18 Guest bedroom
19 Bathroom

The Highest Point

SJB ARCHITECTS

Photography by Peter Clarke and by Tony Miller

With roaring waves below, the steep site for this house required a sensitive approach. "The topography was a challenge. The site was completely covered with natural vegetation. It was fairly difficult, from the outset, to know how the house would appear," says architect Michael Bialek of SJB Architects, who designed this beach house. While the highest point of the site would afford the best views over the ocean and towards the city, it would mean that the house would be subject to some of the strongest winds on the Peninsula. One of the other problems with the site was to provide a protected area for cars. "The wind and the salt air can be fairly unkind to cars' duco," he says.

As a result of selecting the highest point of the site to locate the house, first, it had to be designed in aerofoil. Carrying out wind velocity tests for the structure (in model form), the results suggested a curvaceous room form. Instead of a tiled roof that may not withstand the tumultuous conditions, a corrugated roof was designed. "The wind simply passes over the roof. It was painted grey to merge with the bushland," says Bialek. One of the other main design features to combat the elements was to invert the external walls. Tapering the full-length glass windows into a 30-degree angle not only reduces the effect of strong winds, but also creates a filter for the harsher sunlight.

The owners of this house were clear about the spaces required. "They wanted one large living area with two bedroom wings on either side. A main bedroom, study or retreat and bathroom facilities for themselves, and three bedrooms and bathrooms in the adjoining wing." One of the constraints the site presented was for outdoor entertaining. While the view over the ocean presented some of the liveliest 'theatre' in the area, most would leave the performance midway when faced with the elements. As an alternative, the architects designed the entrance around a more sheltered courtyard. Protected by the natural vegetation and the two bedroom wings, there is some respite from the winds here.

While the clients were confident in SJB Architects from the start, the initial structure caused them some concern. "The steel structure in its bare form looked like a giant whale that had lost its way. It couldn't be compared to other houses they'd come across."

This house first appeared in Domain, in *The Age* newspaper.

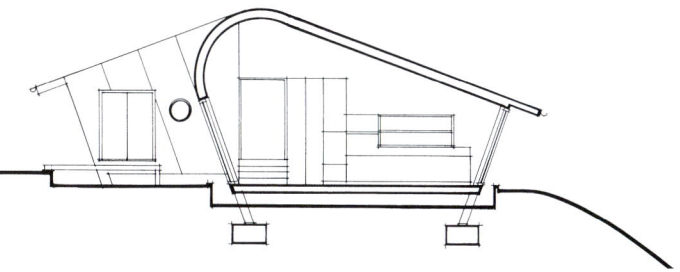

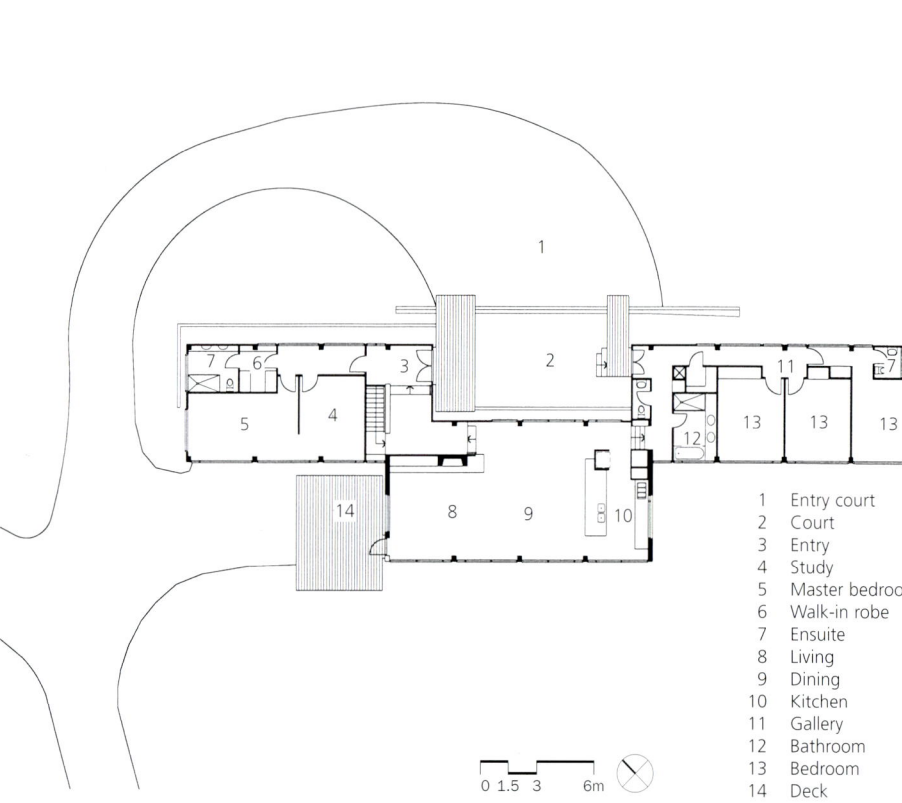

1 Entry court
2 Court
3 Entry
4 Study
5 Master bedroom
6 Walk-in robe
7 Ensuite
8 Living
9 Dining
10 Kitchen
11 Gallery
12 Bathroom
13 Bedroom
14 Deck

0 1.5 3 6m

Once a Cottage
BRUCE RICKARD & ASSOCIATES
Photography by John Gollings

Once a cottage, this house is now a large weekender. The fibro building, owned by architect Bruce Rickard, was fully surrounded by lantana (a noxious shrub that can grow to considerable heights). "I didn't know the property had a view of the water until I climbed an extension ladder against a lemon-scented gum," says Rickard, who decided to take this beach house to the next stage.

Instead of building an entirely new house, Rickard built a large deck extending from the original cottage. With alterations made to the cottage and the new deck, it was the ideal weekender for many years. When the time came to build the new house, the old cottage and deck became integral to the design. The deck was the foundation for the new living/dining/kitchen pavilion, which was designed 2.4 metres higher than, and overlooking the existing lower deck. "My idea with the addition was to convert the old house into bedrooms and build a new freestanding pavilion for the kitchen and living areas." And while the two buildings are clearly distinct, the staircase linking the two structures is fully enclosed.

Like a tent pitched up in the bush, there's a strong sense of the outside from the inside. Rickard used the outdoor timber seating idea from the original deck. Framing the new living spaces, the timber seating can be used for indoor eating or for alfresco dining. The sandstone fireplace in the living area with its timber-lined interior (spotted gum on the walls and brush box on the floors) creates a relaxed feel to the house. "I spent considerable time devising the roof profile, which has a convex-curved ridge and is concave-curved over the eaves. I wanted human-scaled perimeter walls and doors to contrast with the larger-scale pitched space," says Rickard.

On hot summer evenings, the bush takes on a bluish haze. "When you're sitting on the decks, there's a wonderful sense of space. The bush appears to go on indefinitely"

KITCH
DINING
DECK
STUDY

DECK
DINING
KITCHEN
DECK
LIVING
BED1
BED2
BED3
BL
ENTRY
0 1 2 4m

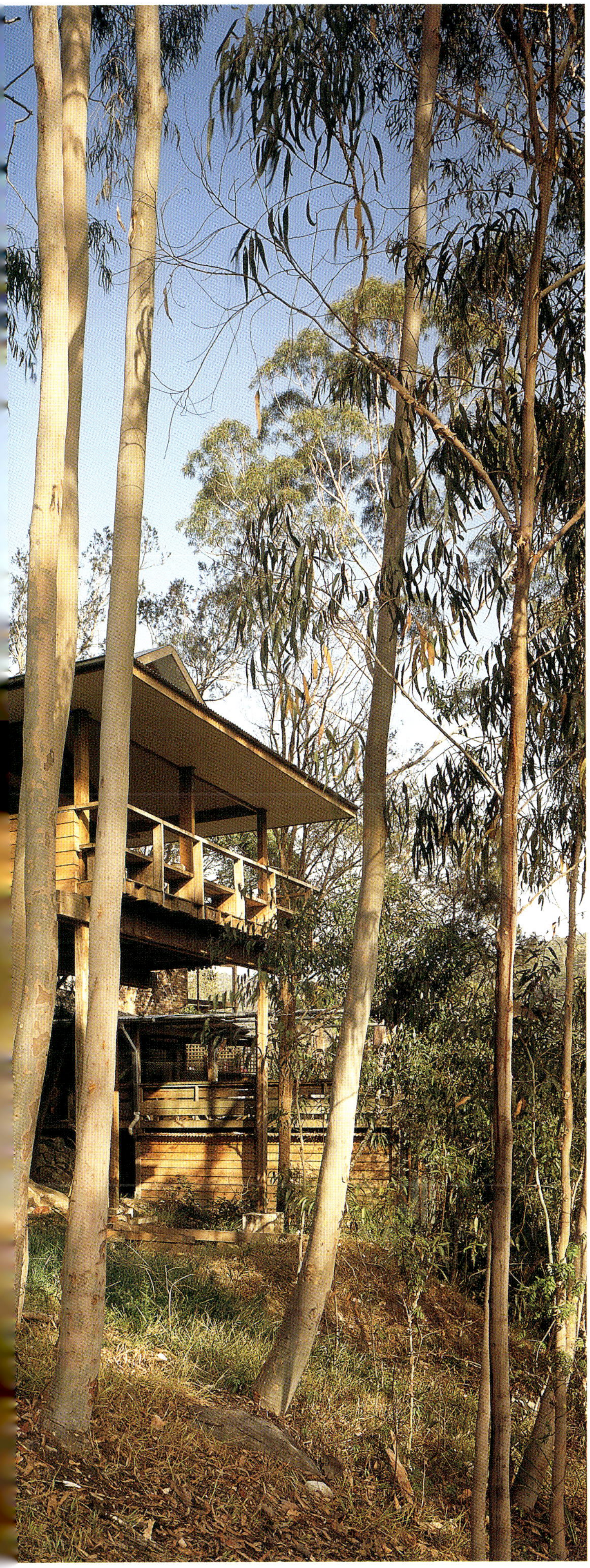

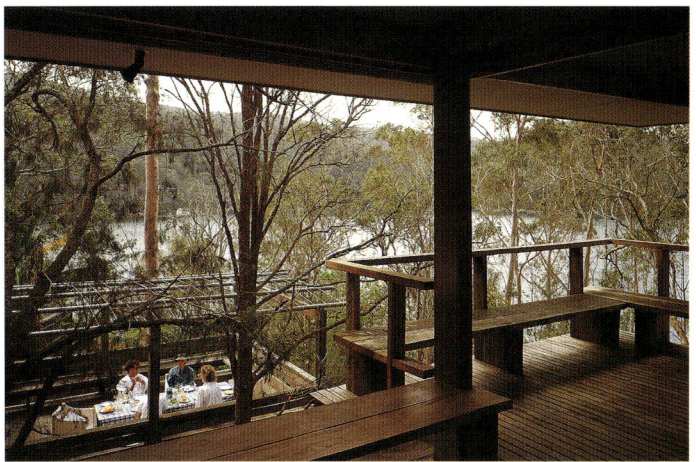

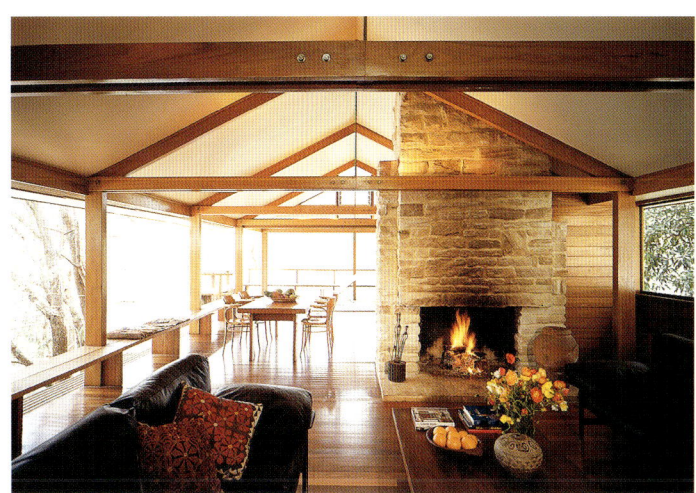

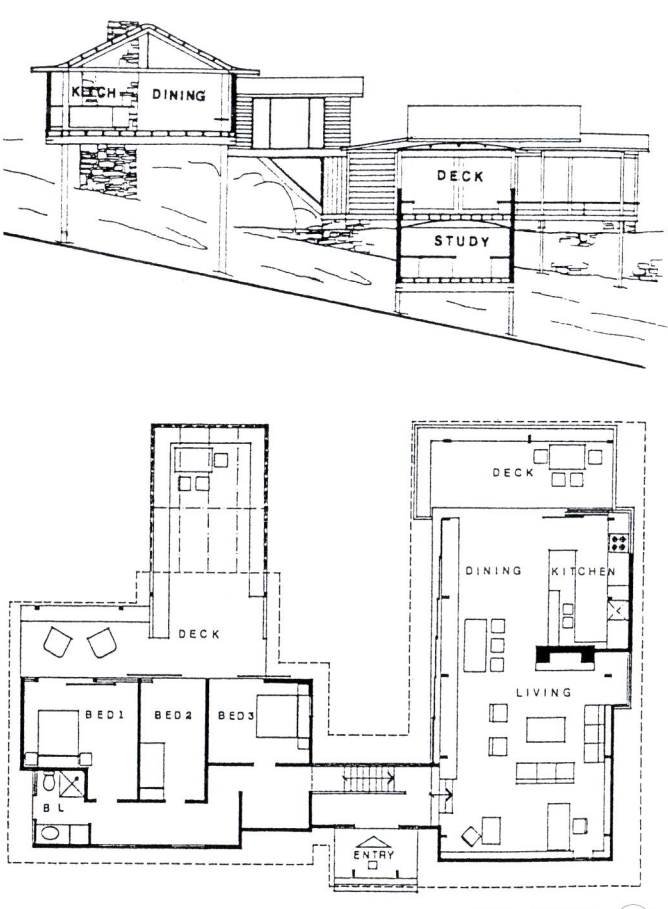

A Sense of Permanence

MELOCCO & MOORE ARCHITECTS
Photography by Liz Cotter

Designed by Melocco & Moore Architects, this striking new beach house is located on the edge of a national park. Originally a vacant site, there's a 3-metre height difference between the front and rear boundary. "It's as if there is a line of force running diagonally across the site (the lower point being at the front)," says architect Phil Moore. The rear and front aspects also differ significantly, with views of the national park to the rear and bay views straight ahead.

The brief for this house was to create 'a sense of permanence'. "My clients wanted a house that was strongly anchored to the site, but which also evoked a holiday feel," says Moore. As a result, the design takes the form of three separate but unified elements. The bedrooms, spread over two levels, are defined within solid concrete-block walls. The heavy masonry provides a sense of sanctuary for the two bedrooms on either level. The second component is the kitchen, dining and living area, defined by the lighter steel-framed, timber-clad wing. The two areas are then brought together by the double-height entry space, containing the staircase. A bridge on the upper level connects the two swings. This central core provides a transparency in the home, evident upon entering.

The rear yard emphasises the dramatic slope of the site. To create the wings and make important connections to the site, Melocco & Moore devised a series of concrete-block retaining walls. "The walls provide a transition between the natural curve of the land and the more rigid nature of the house," says Moore. However, the excavation was used to the architects' advantage. The rear deck area is now level with its elevated rear site. This means that stairs leading to the garden are not required and the outdoor areas can be enjoyed directly from the kitchen. "The bedroom block was deliberately held back. But we brought the main living area forward to maximise the views and catch the breezes," says Moore.

While the house appears to be a large monumental home from the street, its interior spaces are comparatively modest. Approximately 250 square metres, its street presence is largely due to the irregular topography and the contrast between the heavier and lighter elements of the home. And while the home's location can be appreciated from street level, a more impressive image appears at the top of the staircase, where the entire bay can be seen.

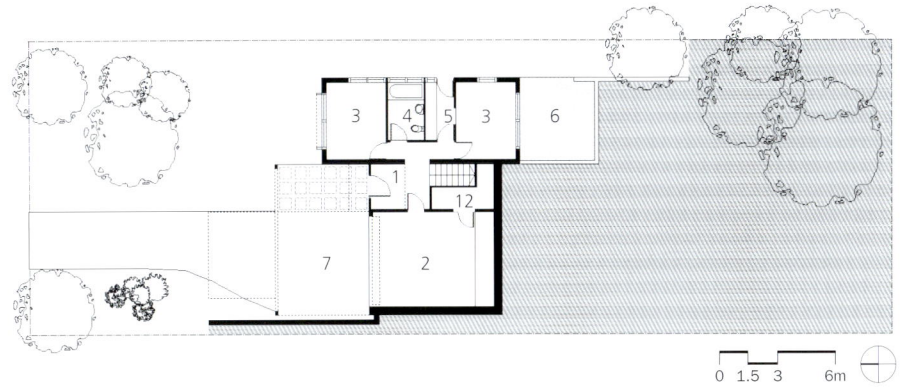

1 Entry
2 Garage
3 Bedroom
4 Bathroom
5 Laundry
6 Courtyard
7 Undercroft
8 Kitchen
9 Dining
10 Living
11 Deck
12 Store
13 Shadehouse

0 1.5 3   6m

97

The Full Brunt of the Weather

HOLAN JOUBERT ARCHITECTS

Photography by Peter Hyatt

This beach house, built on a remote headland, faces the full brunt of the weather. It is blustery and relentless, as the winds come in over the sparse vegetation. The native trees on the site's boundaries form the only protection from the elements. Located on the crest of the hill and with views of the bay, the inclement weather provides great 'theatre' for the owners of this house.

Designed by Holan Joubert Architects, the brief was to create 'the great escape'. The three-storey house includes car parking, a laundry and storage on the ground level, two bedrooms (one main) and a bathroom on the first level, and an open-plan kitchen, dining and living on the top level (with 360-degree views). The brief for the 'great escape' required the architects to provide something in sharp contrast to the couple's city house. "They didn't want us to design a replica of all the things they surround themselves with in the city. They wanted something that was more austere, where the location rather than all the usual trappings could be appreciated," says Holan. As a result, the interior of the three-tiered house is extremely simple and almost monastic in its austerity. There are few decorative elements. "We wanted to focus on the view and create something that they wouldn't experience in the city," he says.

Precision double-glazing completely seals the house from the strong winds. And to ensure the views can be appreciated from many vantage points, the architects designed fully glazed internal doors. While the plastic and steel staircases running through the three levels are only semi-translucent, they do allow the view rather than the interior to dominate. BHP custom orb Colorbond was used for the walls, together with steel and glass. "These materials are familiar to coastal buildings. The plastic is perhaps part of a new architectural language for the 21st century," says Holan, who also used plastic to construct the water tanks on either side of the house.

The clients had no preconceived ideas of the beach house and what it should look like. As Holan says, "They made the remark when it was completed that it was 'nothing like they expected or had seen anywhere before.'"

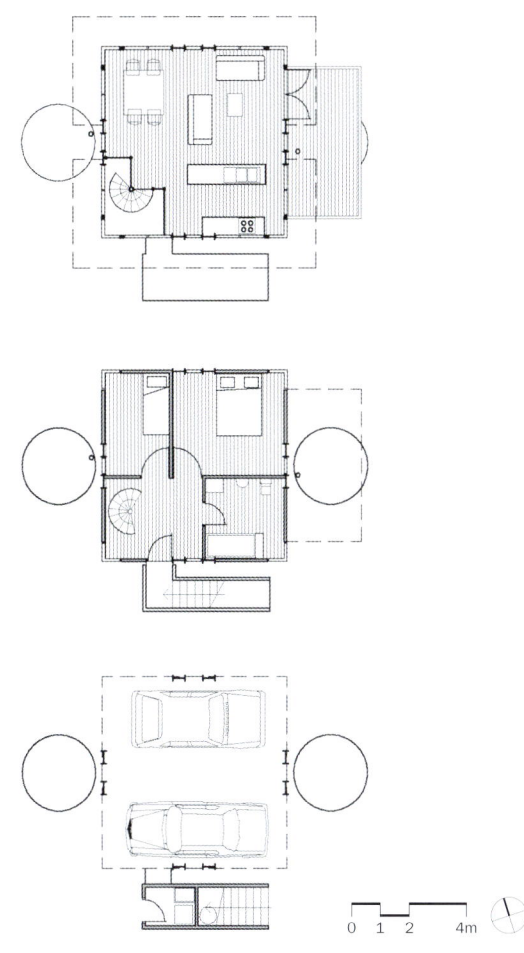

Wedged in

STUTCHBURY & PAPE ARCHITECTS

Photography by Patrick Bingham Hall and by Julie Phipps

On the edge of a ridgeline, this beach house overlooks the ocean and rocky coastline. It also overlooks headlands, a peninsula and a forest, as well as the bay. For Stutchbury & Pape Architects, these multiple views shaped the design of the house.

Designed as two intersecting triangles, the house not only addresses the conditions of the site, but also takes in the views from all directions. "We wanted to acknowledge each of the four aspects, the beach, the headlands, the peninsula and the bay," says architect Peter Stutchbury.

At the junction of the two wedges the entry is defined. On the lower level, there's the children's bedrooms, play area and bathroom facilities. On the main level, there's the main kitchen, dining and living areas, complete with a large triangular deck. And forming the other triangle on the upper level is the main bedroom and ensuite.

The rear triangular structure is solid. Made of concrete and reverse brick veneer, it is embedded well into the landscape. The front triangular spaces are constructed in a timber frame. "The front section is part of the much greater landscape," says Stutchbury. The different aspects of the landscape can be appreciated as one moves through the house. "We made very considered and strategic changes in the design that captured the differences between the land and sky emotions," he says.

The slatted timber exterior wall captures the context of the forest. The spacing of the timber slats becomes closer as one moves nearer to the forest. As Stutchbury says, "We didn't see the house simply as a building, but as a sculptural form, emerging from the forest."

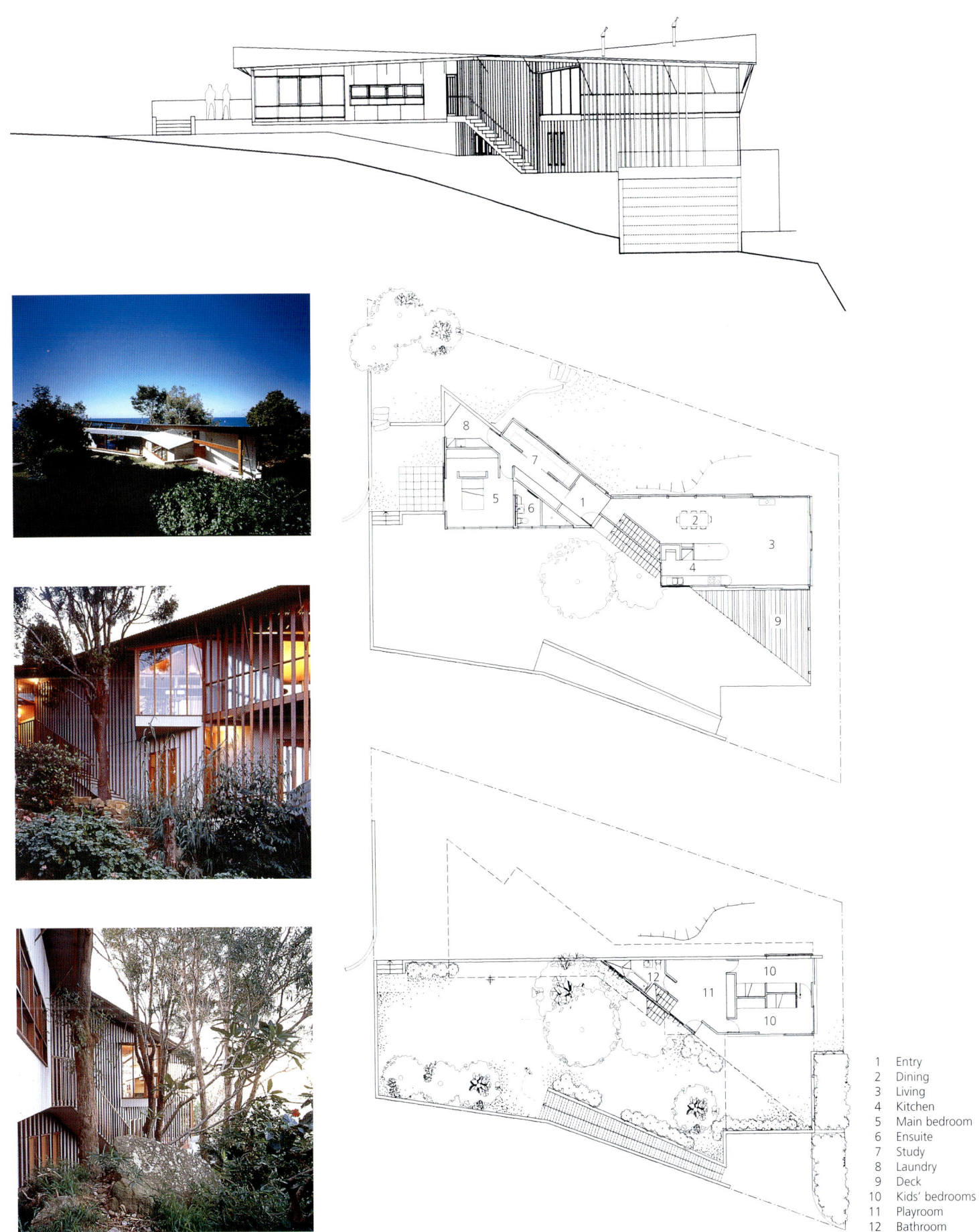

1 Entry
2 Dining
3 Living
4 Kitchen
5 Main bedroom
6 Ensuite
7 Study
8 Laundry
9 Deck
10 Kids' bedrooms
11 Playroom
12 Bathroom

Leaving the Suburbs Behind
MOLNAR FREEMAN ARCHITECTS
Photography by Patrick Bingham-Hall

This timber beach house overlooking the surf, seems as if it's miles from anywhere, even though there's a suburban feel to the street. The owners bought two blocks of land here and, abutting a reserve, the site turns its back on the street. "There's only one immediate neighbour. As soon as you enter the driveway, suburbia is left behind," says architect Katie Molnar.

Designed by Molnar Freeman Architects, this large beach house overlooks a surf beach. Elevated on a rock platform, the weather conditions can be unpredictable. "The location required a solid house (to counter the wind), but the clients didn't want an imposing and monumental house. They wanted something that appeared lightweight, typical of many of the houses along the coast," says Molnar. While it's not apparent, the architects used a 'reverse veneer' technique, bricks on the inside and timber cladding on the outside. The recycled white mahogany timber will turn grey over time and merge with the local banksias. As Molnar explains, "Using this technique is thermally ideal. It's also a solid construction, which is essential for the area."

To reduce the scale of the house, the architects designed it as two separate pavilions. One pavilion houses three bedrooms on the ground level, with the kitchen, living and dining areas above (including a generous wrap-around balcony overlooking the sea). In the other pavilion, there's the children's games room below and the main bedroom and ensuite above. "We didn't want to overpower the bush. The two wings not only reduce the scale of the house, but are also closely aligned with the contours of the land," says Molnar. "We wanted to ensure that there was immediate access to the outside from every part of the house," she adds. There's a protected courtyard outside the games room and generous decks were designed on the first level."

While there's always activity in the street, from inside this house the only noise that can be heard is the sound of crashing waves.

1 Kitchen
2 Dining
3 Deck
4 Living
5 Void
6 W.C.
7 Ensuite
8 Bedroom
9 Laundry
10 Bathroom
11 Courtyard
12 Entry
13 Games room

Opening to the Views

KERSTIN THOMPSON ARCHITECTS

Photography by Patrick Bingham-Hall

The only thing that's precious about this beach house is the time spent in it. This weekender, designed by Kerstin Thompson Architects is a building that would allow the owners the freedom to enjoy their weekend, without worrying about scuffs on the walls.

Made of tilt-slab concrete, the house appears as an extension of the cobbled driveway that leads to the front door. The bleached colour of the concrete compliments the sandy ground that the house occupies. To maximise the views to the sea and the natural light, bedrooms were placed on the ground level, and the kitchen and living areas, together with the main bedroom, were designed on the first level of the house. A roof terrace occupies the third level. Approximately 18 square metres in size, the client's brief was for a spacious warehouse by the sea. With a building height of 7.5 metres above natural ground level, creating three levels to capture the views posed a challenge. To overcome this constraint, the architects varied the ceiling heights. The ceiling height (3 metres) is lower on the ground floor. For the middle level, the ceiling heights are more generous at 4.5 metres. These differentiations allowed for the construction of a roof deck on the third level.

Rather than superfluous window treatments and complicated joinery, large glass picture windows in tilt-slab concrete create a wider and sharper view of the surrounding bushland and sea. And when the owners arrive, the house can be opened up to the environment through a series of doors. "When the house isn't occupied, the building becomes an uncommonly neat box," says architect Kerstin Thompson. "The large sliding doors are opened up on arrival and then the interior becomes part of the balcony space. On leaving, it almost folds back on itself," she says. The glazed tilt doors and sliding doors not only provide important connections to the landscape, but also create important cross-flow ventilation by taking advantage of the sea breeze. "The living areas become like virtual verandahs when they are opened up," says Thompson.

The interior was also kept relatively simple and streamlined. The tilt-slab panels were deliberately left unlined. Even the steel bolts used to construct the house have been left exposed. There's no attempt to dress up the concrete and make it appear like something it isn't. While many homes built as weekenders can take months and sometimes years to complete, this home was constructed in a number of days. One neighbour several streets away, was slightly alarmed by this new home. "He woke one morning and found this building had gone up literally overnight," says Thompson.

Sharing Time

HOLAN JOUBERT ARCHITECTS

Photography by Marc Phee Photography

For a couple with children, living in the inner city, this beach house is a welcome retreat. Instead of being hemmed in by neighbours, the closest thing to their doorstep is the native scrub. A five-minute walk from the protected beach, time spent at the beach house often extends beyond the weekend. "Time is shared between the two houses," says architect Daniel Holan, of Holan Joubert Architects who co-designed the house.

On a long narrow site (17 by 50 metres), the 230-square-metre house is divided into three zones. To one side of the house is the children's wing (two bedrooms and a television room). The lounge, kitchen and dining area occupies the central zone. And on the other side of the house are the main bedroom, bathroom and study. Two corridors on either side of the main living area accentuate the three divisions. Unlike many city terraces, with long dark corridors, these passageways are light and well ventilated. Louvred glass windows designed at both ends of the house allow for the continuous flow of sea breezes through the house.

As one of the owners is tall (over 2 metres), the architects were mindful of providing generous ceiling heights. In the main living area, the pitched ceiling extends from 4.5 metres to 4.7 metres in height. Even in the bedrooms, the ceilings are 3.4 metres high. "We wanted to make strong connections to the bush and create a sense of transparency. The idea wasn't to feel as though you were living in a bunker," says Holan. Large glass doors at either end of the kitchen/living area can be pulled right back on warmer days.

The beach house features a stained plywood skin, detailed with timber battens. The stained plywood cedar is a refreshing alternative to many of the palettes used for beach houses. "It's a beach house, but that doesn't mean you need to try and match up the paint colours with the sea," says Holan, who, like the owners, preferred a more sophisticated approach to the scheme. The neutral palette inside the beach house, allows the gnarled bushland to be the focus, together with the massive Oregon beams (250 by 50 millimetres) above the living area. "The beams outline the roof, but they're structurally important to the design," he says.

Sophisticated and restrained, this beach house is also robust. The children have their own areas, but they aren't restricted from enjoying the entire house. And when the doors are pulled back, they can explore the bushland setting freely.

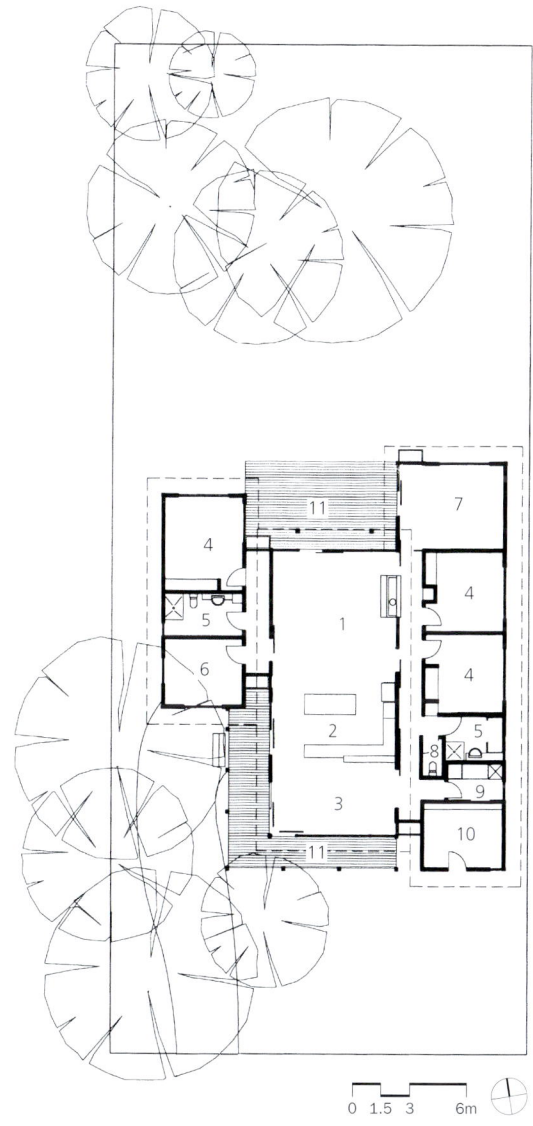

1 Living	7 Sitting
2 Kitchen	8 W.C.
3 Dining	9 Laundry
4 Bedroom	10 Store
5 Bathroom	11 Deck
6 Study	

A Large Viewing Platform
NEVILLE QUARRY ARCHITECT
Photography by Adrian Boddy

Perched on a cliff overlooking a protected inlet, this new beach house is framed by gum trees. Replacing a simple fibro shack, the new house occupies the previous footprint (12 by 20 metres). "My clients wanted a serene sense of enclosure as well as an outlook to the water from every room," says architect Neville Quarry, who designed the house. "They preferred timber and glass, something that would sit among the trees," he adds. In fact, the house sits like a deck between the trees, like a raft, that has found its way onto the shore. Quarry's design has a strong connection to the water. "I've created one horizontal platform, which is partly inside and partly outside. The design is firmly anchored to the ground. But there's a sense of freedom between the trees," he says.

Large blackbutt tresses support the house while hoop pine features on the exterior of the house, as well as on the deck areas. The roof, made of corrugated steel, was designed as a single plane canopy and is slightly tilted to capture the view. Internal walls extend to become exterior walls, not only connecting to the outdoor spaces, but also creating privacy and controlling the light. Highlight windows in the main living area frame the view of the bush. "The sun is received in all directions. The light has a wonderful effect at all times of the day. There's quite a dramatic shift with the shadows," says Quarry.

The elevated platform includes the kitchen, dining and living areas. There are also a main bedroom and a bathroom on the first floor. The lower level houses two guest bedrooms, a bathroom and an artist's studio (for the owner). While the bush views and the water views are magical, Quarry was also keen to include a third element. The architect designed one large gutter to collect all the rainwater. Once gathered, the rainwater is discharged via a mesh stainless-steel structure. With the size of the gutter, the leaves and debris cascade over the mesh. "It's a functional sculpture. The owners can enjoy the movement of the leaves as well as the ripples of the water," says Quarry.

117

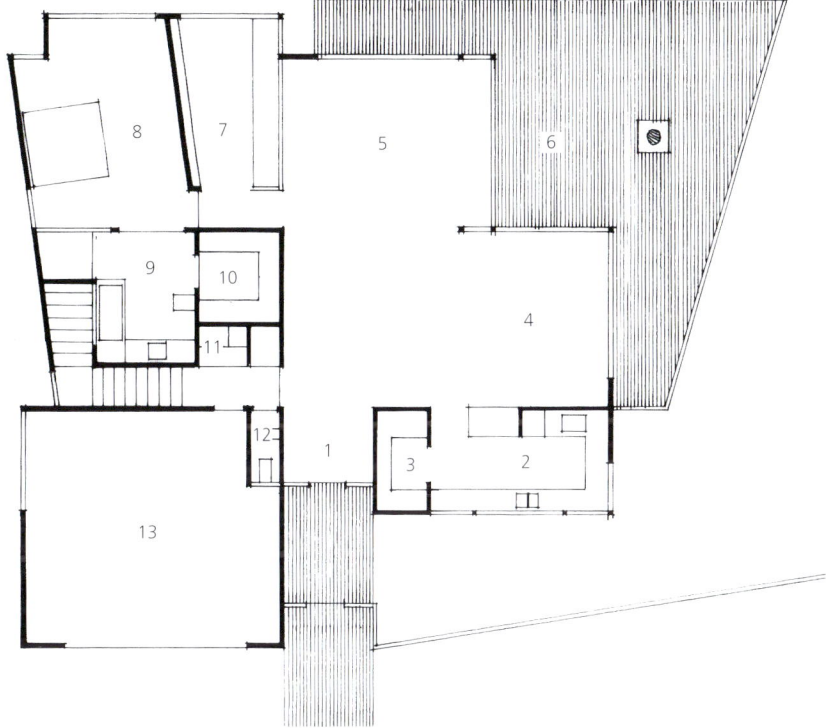

1 Entry
2 Kitchen
3 Pantry
4 Dining
5 Living
6 Deck
7 Library
8 Bedroom
9 Bathroom
10 Dressing room
11 Laundry
12 W.C.
13 Garage

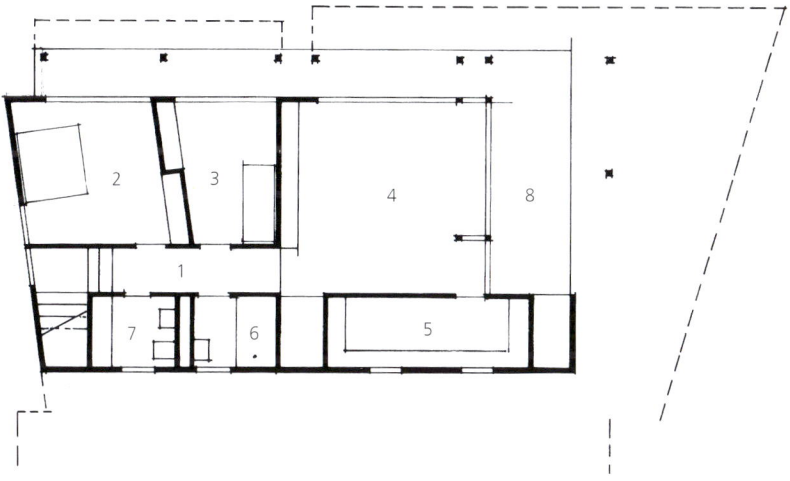

1   Hall
2&3 Bedroom
4   Studio
5   Storage
6   Shower
7   W.C.
8   Terrace

Manipulating the Site

CONNOR + SOLOMON ARCHITECTS

Photography by Ken Brass and Paul Connor

Located on a steep escarpment, overlooking a magnificent coastline, both the architects and their clients were keen to maximise the views to the sea and headlands. Designed by Connor + Solomon Architects, this large new house on the water's edge seems to continue indefinitely. While the house appears to have been commissioned for a large family, it was actually designed for a couple, whose children and grandchildren come to stay on a regular basis.

This large rendered home occupies most of the 400-square-metre site. The shape of the site also made the architect's task more difficult. "Our clients wanted views from all the spaces, but it's quite an unusual site. The shape is similar to two flags, which have been joined together (the site is only 6 metres in width at the centre)," says architect Paul Connor. To obtain as many sea views as possible, Connor + Solomon designed a courtyard pool in the centre of the site. They also located the couple's main bedroom and living areas at the front of the site, with the main bedroom and ensuite facilities on the first floor, taking in the panoramic views. However, even from the stairs, nooks and landings within the house, the architects ensured water views. "There are also glimpses of the beach from most windows. We made sure there was an outlook from the study too, where the owner spends a reasonable amount of time," says Connor. "We wanted to create a series of spaces that differ at various times of the day," he says.

The house was inspired by many of the buildings the architects had seen on their travels, in particular the Moorish architecture of Spain. "I showed my clients this book I had on the Balearic Islands. They had an instant affinity with the images," says Connor. "The old house (which was pulled down) had a turret." There are also a series of turreted houses close by. To pay homage to the past and to the house's context, this home incorporates a tower as well. "We like to reflect on the past, but it's also important to create a contemporary statement with a new design," says Connor.

While the view from the tower is spectacular, the views from the large terraces leading from the house are equally impressive.

Sharing the View
CHENCHOW LITTLE ARCHITECTS
Photography by Richard Glover (exterior) and by Anthony Browell (interior)

Originally there was a duplex on this beachfront site. One dwelling on top of the other, only the second-floor duplex had views to the ocean. A small timber cottage, which occupies land in the foreground, is currently in the 'zone of wave impact'. "It could be there for years but it could also be removed by the power of nature," says architect Tony Chenchow, who designed a new duplex behind the cottage with architect Stephanie Little.

Designed for two clients, the brief to Chenchow Little Architects was for a duplex, side by side, rather than one upon the other. "They both wanted three bedrooms (one to be used as a study), open-plan living areas and something which would convey a relaxed type of living," says Chenchow. Designed over three levels, each duplex has a garage and entrance on the ground level, bedrooms on the first level and open-plan living areas on the third level. "We wanted to maximise the views. But we also wanted to create a sculptural roofline and maximise the ceiling heights on the top level," he says.

The angled roofline that extends over the outdoor patios provides a strong contrast to the rectilinear form of the levels below. At 5 metres in height at the highest point, the angled roof creates a double-voided space, similar in feel to many warehouses in the inner city. "It does feel like being in a warehouse. But instead of being situated in a back lane, it's overlooking the beach," says Chenchow.

While each duplex is strongly defined from within, the configuration of each can also be read from the beach. The rendered masonry façade is clearly delineated into two distinct homes by means of vertical blade walls. And while the living areas can be fully exposed to the beach, they can easily be screened by means of retractable timber louvres. "When they're closed, the patios act as another room," says Chenchow.

Both parties can enjoy the beach views. And while it might feel like a warehouse from inside, the sea views are a continual reminder that the city is far away.

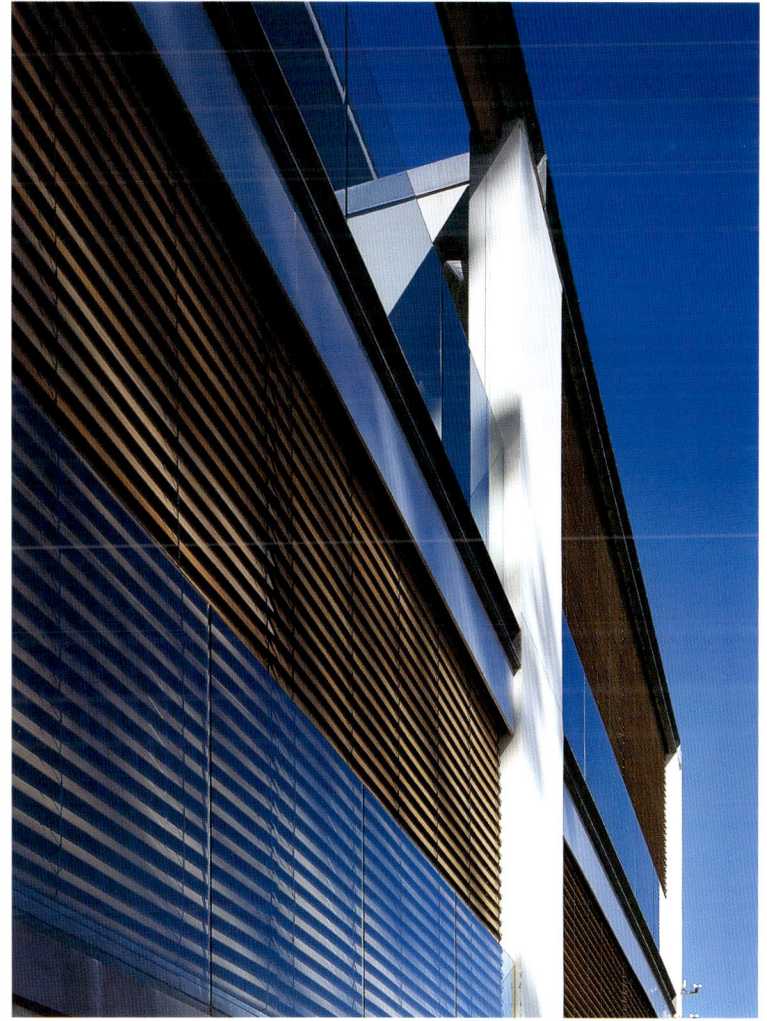

Dwelling One Dwelling Two

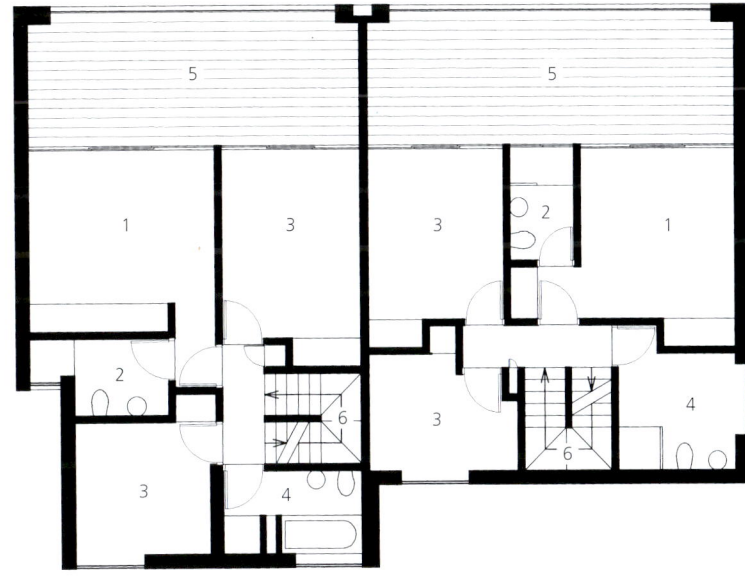

1. Master bedroom
2. Ensuite
3. Bedroom
4. Bathroom
5. Deck
6. Stair
7. Kitchen
8. Living/dining

Maximum Exposure

COL BANDY ARCHITECTS

Photography by Richard Lenartowicz

Given the exposed site, it was understandable that the owners of this weekender wanted a home that was well anchored to the land. "My clients didn't want a house that would 'touch the earth lightly'. With the strong winds, a simple timber structure wouldn't fare too well," says architect Col Bandy, who was commissioned to design the new house. "Thirty per cent of the house is buried into the site. It was important to follow the contours of the site and to reinstate the original contours after the bulldozer had been through," he says.

Along with a brief to maximise the views, it was also important for the owners to capture sunlight within the home. However, one of the main constraints of the site is that the southern views to the water are those most exposed to the elements. While the house is framed with doors to enjoy all aspects, Bandy designed a large central courtyard to add a more protected element to the site. "Sometimes it can rain for a week here. Even if there's only five minutes of sunshine, the whole weekend shouldn't be spoilt by having to stay indoors."

Another main component to the brief was to include three bedrooms for guests who would stay at various times. Instead of designing one bedroom wing in the house, Bandy located the main bedroom suite beyond the kitchen and living areas. The guest's wing is located on the other side of the living area. With floor-to-ceiling glass window-walls to the sea, the beds have been positioned to capture the views. In the main bedroom, which is cantilevered above the rolling grassland, the bed can be swivelled around to take in a number of views. The bathroom facilities offer the same vistas with floor-to-ceiling glass walls in the showers. "The house is isolated up here so it was possible to create a more liberated design. In some respects, the feeling is like going camping and washing next to a river," says Bandy.

Bandy designed one large open pavilion-like space for the living areas. Following the contours of the land, the lounge area is defined by a change of level. When the home's concertina doors are drawn right back in the living room, the courtyard, with its high terracotta walls, acts as another room.

For the owners of this house, predicting the weather doesn't have to be a daily concern. Even if the sun only shines for a few moments at a time, the views can be enjoyed all day long.

This house first appeared in Domain, in *The Age* newspaper.

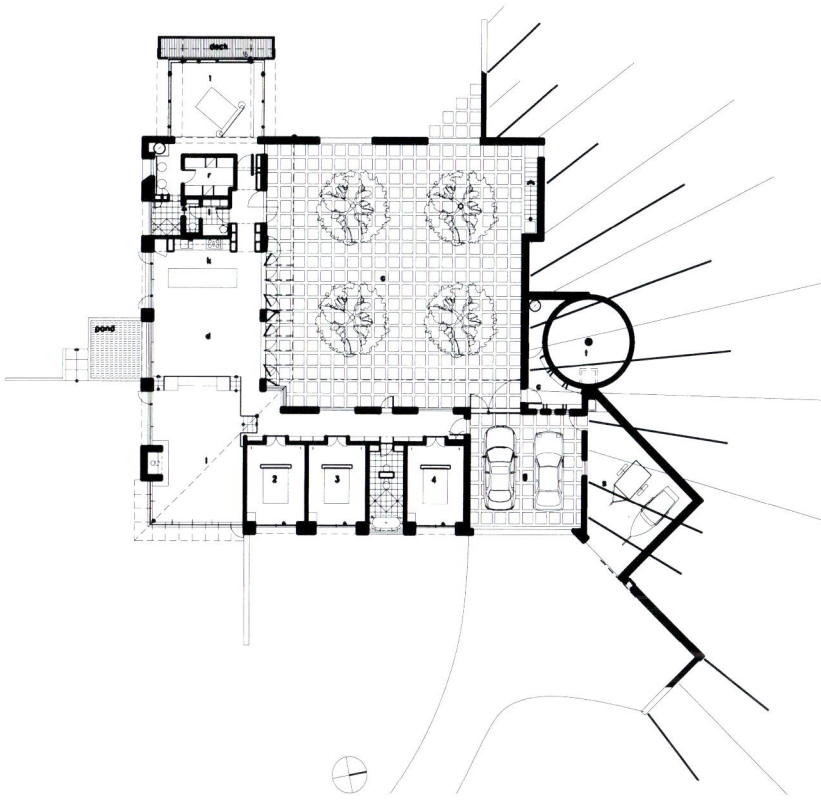

About the Landscape
SWANEY DRAPER ARCHITECTS
Photography by Trevor Mein

This beach house takes a back seat to the view. "It's about the landscape. This house forms a piece of it," says architect Simon Swaney, who designed the house with architect Sally Draper. The beach house, of approximately 400 square metres, was designed above a berm (a man-made shallow escarpment). The front gate that normally defines the boundary of a property has been substituted with the berm.

Treated as rooms, each external space performs a different role. "The deck is the dramatic viewing point. The courtyard is the protected space and the rear is the traditional backyard," says Draper, who was guided by the local climate. "It gets quite cold here, which means that even during a cold wind, you can appreciate the views from a number of outdoor spaces."

The three-level house, made of glass and steel, features a blackbutt timber façade and a 'random rubble' sandstone chimney. Designed for a family with teenage children, the ground level includes the guest wing, laundry and wine cellar. On the first level, there's the main bedroom, ensuite, kitchen and living areas. And on the third level, there's the children's wing, including a separate television area on the level below. The house is clearly expressed as two forms. One is the public space, defined by the glass and steel pavilion at the front. The other component is an enclosed solid with blackbutt timber-clad walls, into which openings are inserted. The two forms are interlocked with a glass louvred breezeway. "We call it the 'link'. The idea was to make as many connections to the outside as possible and to create a variety of experiences from within," says Swaney.

The main living pavilion, with a soaring sandstone fireplace, was designed as one large space. With 5-metre-high ceilings and a band of glass windows/doors, the owners have an uninterrupted view of the water. And weather permitting, the doors to the front patio can be pulled right back. As Swaney says, "The aim is to enjoy the views, the spaces and the bush."

This house first appeared in Domain, in *The Age* newspaper.

1 Hall
2 Bedroom
3 Bathroom
4 Stair
5 Deck
6 Bunkroom
7 Courtyard
8 Ensuite
9 Void (living below)
10 Void
11 Walk-in robe
12 W.C.
13 Study
14 Balcony
15 Living
16 Linen
17 Store
18 Walkway
19 Courtyard
20 Bedroom 1 over bedroom 2 below
21 Kitchen
22 Dining
23 Entry
24 Pond
25 Cellar
26 Laundry
27 Powder room
28 Service yard
29 Garage
30 Forecourt
31 Driveway

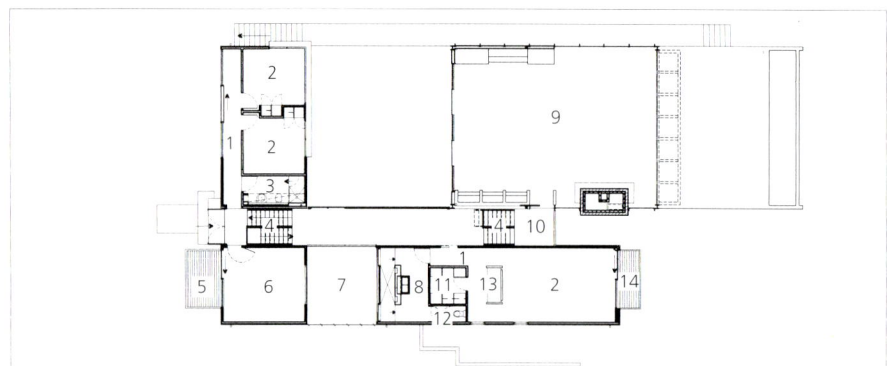
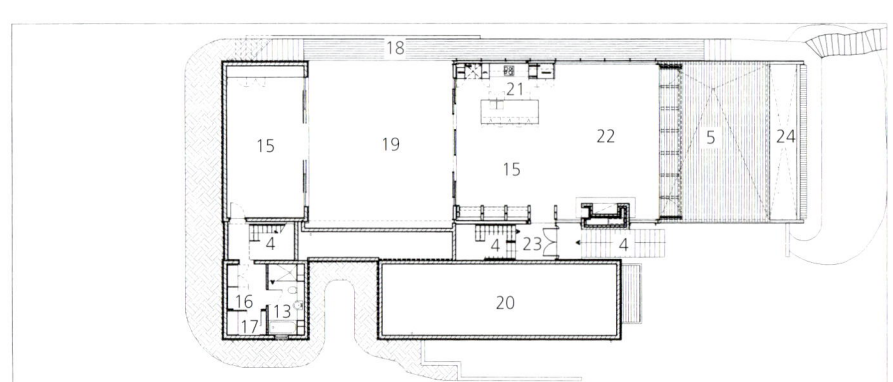
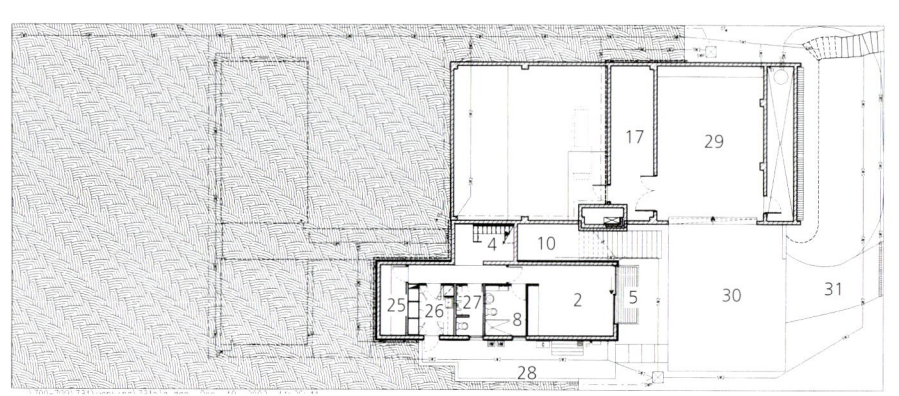

A Small Village

PAUL UHLMANN ARCHITECTS

Photography by David Sandison

This small coastal community consists of only approximately 100 houses. While relatively small in overall size, the ratio of buildings to land is fairly high. Overlooking a park reserve and the ocean, this beach house occupies one of the premier sites. With a 3-metre fall towards the beach, views of the water are found from all vantage points within the home, including the main bedroom on the ground floor.

Designed by Paul Uhlmann Architects, this large house was built for a family with four children, who each needed their own space. The five bedrooms (including the main bedroom) are located on the ground floor, together with a family/recreation room for the children. On the first floor, there are more formal living areas, the kitchen and deck areas. "Creating two zones, one for children and one for parents, was an important part of the brief," says architect Paul Uhlmann.

The house is made of timber chamfer boards and shiplap timber and was deliberately designed to evoke a sense of an Irish village (reminiscent of one of the owner's family home). The timber, stained a weathered grey, will eventually fade. "It's a slightly raw feel, particularly with the dry stacked stone-wall fencing," says Uhlmann. With the home's skillion roofs, there's also a sense of the local vernacular—beach houses built in the 1950s and sixties.

Screening features strongly in this house. The main bedroom, facing the ocean, includes a small courtyard, screened from the street. On warmer evenings the doors can be left open and the sea breeze can filter into the bedroom. The main staircase also includes timber lattice-like screens on either side of the treads. "It acts as a balustrade and structural support. The open screens also allow the light and air to filter into the downstairs rooms," says Uhlmann.

Creating a house that would be environmentally sensitive was an important aspect to this design. The house is run on solar power, there are water tanks underground and fittings, such as the electric light fitting, were designed with energy efficiency in mind. And while the timber screens add a decorative element to the house, they also provide important cross-ventilation, particularly during the warmer months.

In keeping with the honesty and simplicity of the materials, the floorboards are waxed rather than polished. A few years down the track, both the interior and exterior woodwork will have that slightly worn feel. And bringing sand into the house from the beach will only add to that charm.

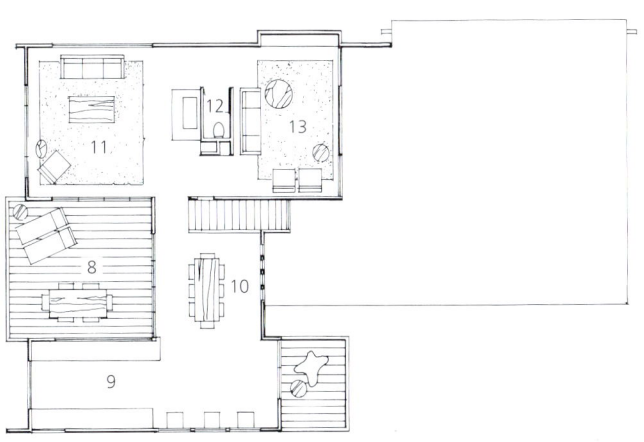
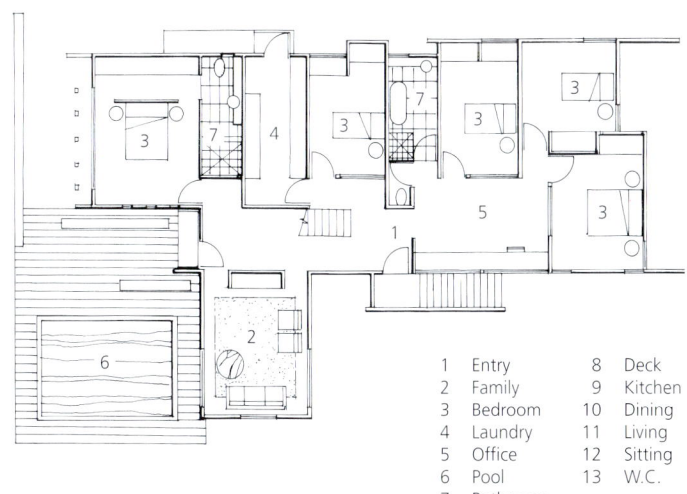

1	Entry	8	Deck
2	Family	9	Kitchen
3	Bedroom	10	Dining
4	Laundry	11	Living
5	Office	12	Sitting
6	Pool	13	W.C.
7	Bathroom		

Protection from the Wind

**DESIGN KING COMPANY
IN ASSOCIATION WITH PETER IRELAND ARCHITECT**

Photography by Brett Boardman

This beach house, designed by architects Jon King and Peter Ireland, is located in a hostile environment. Fronting the Pacific Ocean, gale-force south-easterly winds buffet the house for a significant part of the year. "Some houses have been lost in the area (the sea and the dunes reclaiming their territory)," says King.

The client's brief was to replace a fibro shack with a completely new house, one that would take advantage of the views. "The shack was low down in the dunes. There was very little sense of context," he adds. The architects created a new platform for living, one that skimmed the top of the dunes. As a result, the ceiling in the living areas, extending into the bedrooms, is made from strong curve-shaped plywood. "The curl wraps back over itself in the bedrooms to create added security," says King.

The H-shaped plan of the house had to be flexible. The clients wanted an office, holiday retreat and a permanent residence. Not sure if their alliance was to the city or the coast, the design had to accommodate indecisiveness. Two studies can be used for bedrooms should additional guests stay over. The architects also provided a number of alternative outdoor areas for their clients. "A large deck overlooking the ocean is the common formula when designing beach houses. But often people need protective outdoor spaces which allow them to move out of the wind," says King. For this house a number of side courtyards were designed. Sheltered from the wind, they can be used for greater parts of the year.

While the house appears to lightly float over the dunes, it is well anchored on the site. Large concrete piles extend into the substratum, 16 metres below ground level. However, as a result of the concrete columns, the sand can still move freely below.

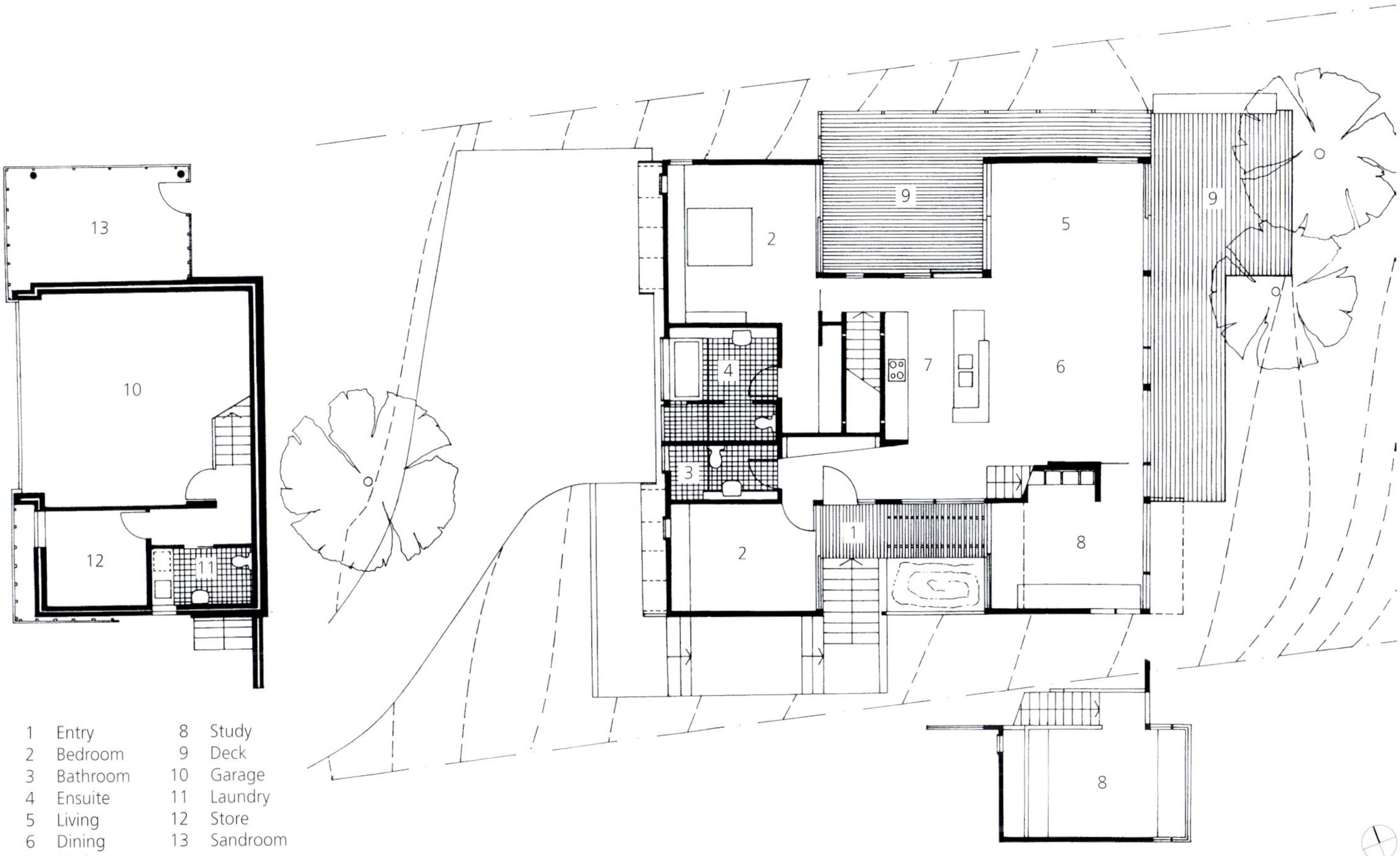

1	Entry	8	Study
2	Bedroom	9	Deck
3	Bathroom	10	Garage
4	Ensuite	11	Laundry
5	Living	12	Store
6	Dining	13	Sandroom
7	Kitchen		

A New Form
PAUL UHLMANN ARCHITECTS
Photography by David Sandison

Surrounded by palatial homes, many of which are three and four storeys, this beach house is by comparison relatively modest. "In an area of brand new homes, the original 1980s home was probably one of the oldest," says architect Paul Uhlmann, who recently redesigned this house with a more contemporary edge.

Originally designed to accommodate two families who could live independently from each other, the brief was to create one home. "They were completely detached. The courtyard in the centre of the two homes was the main connection," says Uhlmann. A number of walls were demolished and the courtyard was completely transformed. A plunge pool (complete with a square porthole window) was designed for the courtyard, framed by a river-stone wall. A significant part of the courtyard was also enclosed with full-length opaque glass doors. Now used as a secondary living area for the family, it's difficult to imagine the home's original structure. "We wanted to retain part of the courtyard. The south-easterly trade winds can make the conditions on the beachside quite blustery. It's important to have an alternative outdoor area for four to five months of the year," says Uhlmann.

The 1980s home had a low ceiling. Currently, in part of the informal living area (facing the beach), the ceiling height is only 2.7 metres. "I like this scale. It creates a sheltered feeling from within. There's a sense of intimacy," says Uhlmann. However, to make the most of its idyllic position, Paul Uhlmann Architects installed large timber and glass sliding doors that can be completely pulled back. The side glass louvred windows can manipulate the prevailing winds. To compensate for the low roof and to give the home a new focal point, the architects included four recycled timber beams for the beach façade. "They provide structural support," he adds.

While the house is often occupied by more than one family, the spaces can now be shared by everyone.

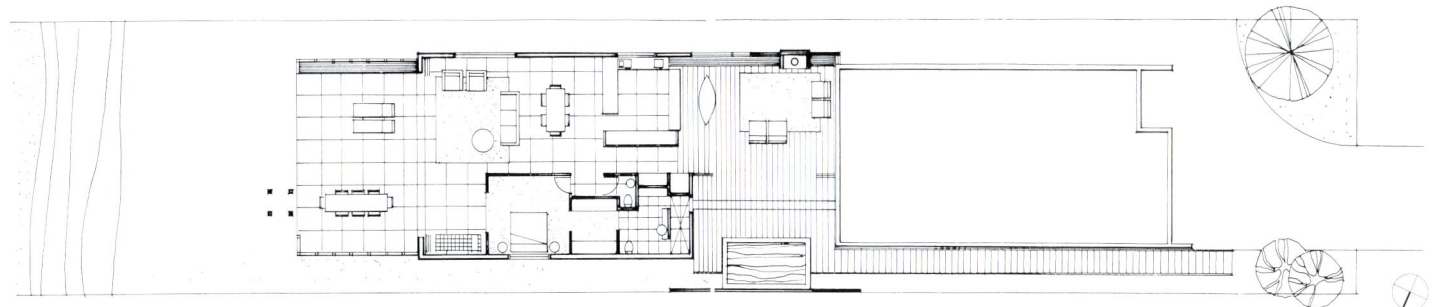

180-Degree Views

ARCHITECTS INK
Photography by Trevor Fox

To capitalise on the ocean views, this house was designed at the rear of the site. With a 20 per cent gradient, the view was improved with every metre further back from the front boundary. As the client's brief was to maximise the views, this placement would allow for 180-degree views of the ocean.

Designed by Architects Ink, this beach house is made of concrete block work and a compressed fibro-cement board that resembles weatherboard. "We wanted to emphasise it was a beach shack rather than a house in a suburb," says architect Marco Spinelli, who worked on the house with architect Giovina Lippis. The architects were keen to contrast the materials between the heavier block work and the lighter cement boards and metal sheeting for the roof. In contrast to the block work, which acts as a plinth or anchor in the design, the lightweight awnings and roofline seem to soar above the site. "The contrast provides a sense of floating," says Spinelli.

The cantilevered awnings diffuse the morning light and extend the views from within the house, which includes those from all four bedrooms and living areas. The two bedrooms and the rumpus room on the ground floor are separated from the main bedroom and second bedroom on the first floor. Designed for one family, the house also provides ideal accommodation for two families who also want their own space. The arrangement of spaces has been carefully conceived. The main bedroom and living area on the first floor were designed with generous outdoor patios. All the bedroom and living areas have a view. The kitchen and service areas have more indirect views of the ocean and segmented glimpses of the hills behind.

To reduce the more intense afternoon heat, the rear façade of this house was designed with small windows, which punctuate the building. Keen to include a water feature from all elevations, the architects designed an ingenious concrete boxed gutter into the roof structure. Cantilevered over the dining room window, which has views to neighbouring homes, there is a gentle cascade of water during the wetter periods of the year. "It's more like a waterfall when there's a heavy downpour," says Spinelli. And when it's not raining, the slot-like windows in the dining area capture picture-like vistas over the hillsides. The concrete bulkhead, which makes an indentation into the ceiling, separates the kitchen from the dining room.

Adding to the holiday ambience of the house, the front door is painted a punchy lime-green. Like a welcome mat, there's a sense of arrival and pleasure that starts at the front door.

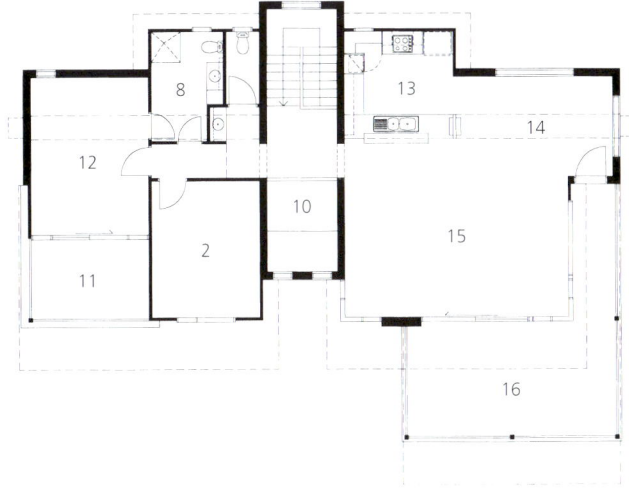

1 Entry
2 Bedroom
3 Rumpus room
4 Terrace
5 Service
6 Laundry
7 Store
8 Bathroom
9 Garage
10 Void
11 Balcony
12 Main bedroom
13 Kitchen
14 Dining
15 Living
16 Deck

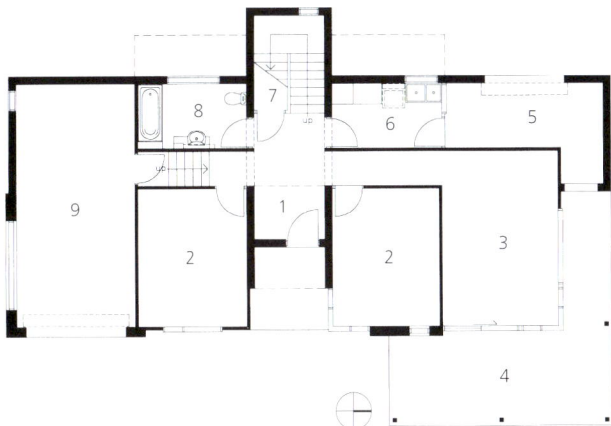

Out to Sea

GREGORY BURGESS ARCHITECTS
Photography by Trevor Mein

Designed by Gregory Burgess Architects, this house was the result of a limited competition. A number of architects were short-listed and asked to submit a scheme. The 10-acre cliff site, overlooking the bay, would have created an adrenalin rush for most of the competing architects.

Before submitting plans for this idyllic site, Burgess, who won the competition, workshopped a number of ideas with the owners. They wanted an extended beach house, which would accommodate three generations of the one family, either at the same time or independently. Unlike many houses, which include only the one main bedroom, this house was designed with four main bedrooms and accompanying ensuite bathrooms (two on the ground level and two on the first floor). "They also wanted separate areas for the children to play, but without isolating these areas," says architect Gregory Burgess.

Therefore, the three main living areas – the breakfast 'plate', the living area and deck, and the dining room – wrap around the kitchen area. The 'fire pit' in the living area, further delineates the open-plan living areas.

Burgess chose to site the house on the cliff face to provide the most dramatic outlook possible. "The house is at the edge where the land starts to gradually fall away (there's a 30.5-metre drop to the bay below). We wanted the house to engage with the eastern edge, as if it was coming out of a wave," says Burgess. The radially sawn yellow stringy-bark house, detailed with galvanised-steel balconies and handrails, features a flat-sheet galvanised-steel lookout. Reminiscent of a ship, the house has a strong prow-like quality. "There's a sense that the house is cutting through the waves," he says.

In contrast to the more lightweight stringy-bark, which was designed to weather, the house features a low solid limestone wall, meandering to the home's entrance. "The wall is similar to an anchor. It creates a sense of stability and directs you towards the main entrance or vestibule," says Burgess. Instead of the entrance being clearly visible from the front of the house, Burgess 'buries' it. "The limestone wall drags you into the house and then you can start peeling off the layers once you're inside."

Like a ship, with a number of decks to explore, the generous landings and internal courtyards follow the contours of the land. And while there is an intriguing series of paths to follow, one of the most worn is the one that leads to the pool and spa area. The loose shade structure, covering the spa and partially covering the pool, appears like a palm frond that has just been brought home from the beach. Made of yellow stringy-bark, it creates dappled shade across the deck. While the sea is 30.5 metres below, the house has an aerodynamic presence. There is a sense of it cutting through the water at great speed.

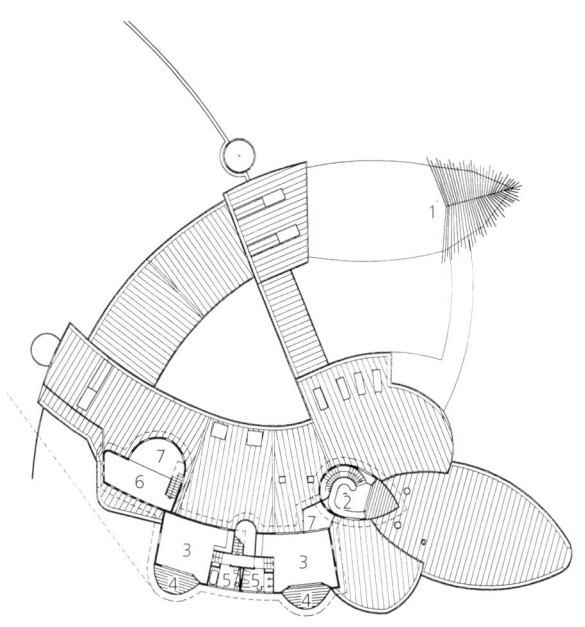

1	Canopy
2	Lookout
3	Master bedroom
4	Balcony
5	Bathroom
6	Loft
7	Void

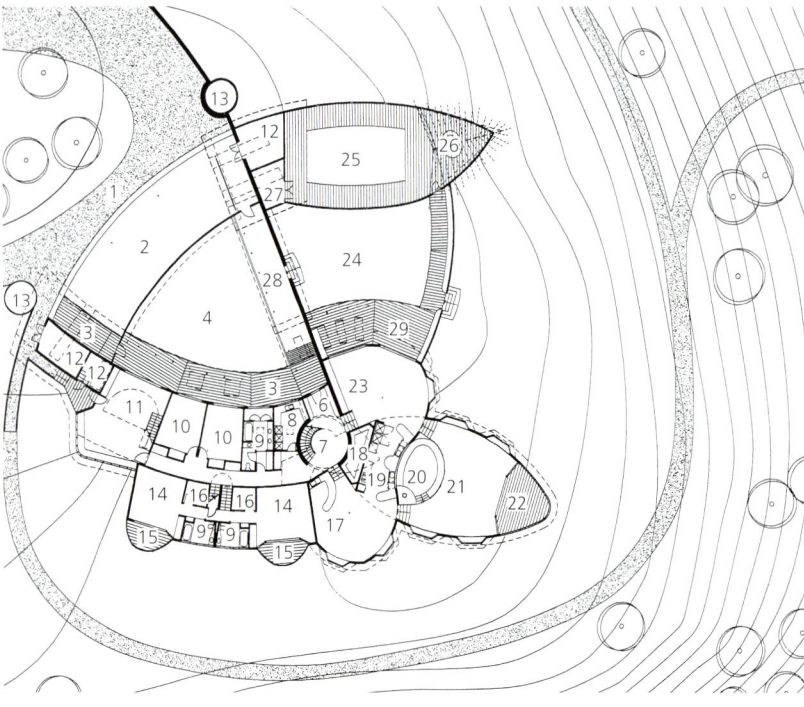

1	Driveway
2	Carport
3	Ramp
4	Courtyard
5	Verandah
6	Entry
7	Verstible
8	Laundry
9	Bathroom
10	Bedroom
11	Rumpus
12	Store
13	Rainwater tank
14	Master bedroom
15	Balcony
16	Alcove
17	Dining
18	Pantry
19	Kitchen
20	Firepit
21	Living
22	Deck
23	Breakfast
24	Terrace
25	Pool
26	Spa
27	Pool equipment
28	Walkway
29	Barbeque

A Roof with a View

NORMAN DAY + ASSOCIATES

Photography by Shannon Pawsey

This coastal village, developed in the 1920s and thirties, is two hours drive from the city. "Most of the houses in the area are concealed shacks in the bush. Many of the original beach houses have been retained. But my clients were looking for something contemporary," says architect Norman Day.

Day's clients were keen to build not one house, but three. They wanted to live in one and sell the remaining two. It was clear from the start that the established model of the concealed shack in the bush was not going to be appropriate. "We proposed a different model, more akin to the type of development you would find in a Mediterranean village," says Day, who was keen to include elements such as roof decks in the design.

The three houses (approximately 250 square metres each), all have their own rooftop decks. Each has bedrooms on the ground floor, the kitchen and living areas in the middle level and roof decks above. Traditionally, bedrooms are placed on the upper levels of a house. But in this case, the architect was keen to establish a closer relationship between the living areas and the outdoor spaces above. "The light is better from the second level and there are also views of the bay," says Day.

Made of Villa Board and a waterproof plywood (used for boat building), the houses feature a glass tower, enclosing the stairwell that leads to the roof decks. "You can see the outline of people moving up and down the stairs. The shadows activate the houses," he adds. The locals were initially concerned regarding privacy issues and the density of the development. But Day included screens on the roof decks to create privacy and to screen the sunlight. And like the colours found in the Mediterranean, Day used three different cement-washed colours to delineate each house; one in purple, one in ochre and one in umber.

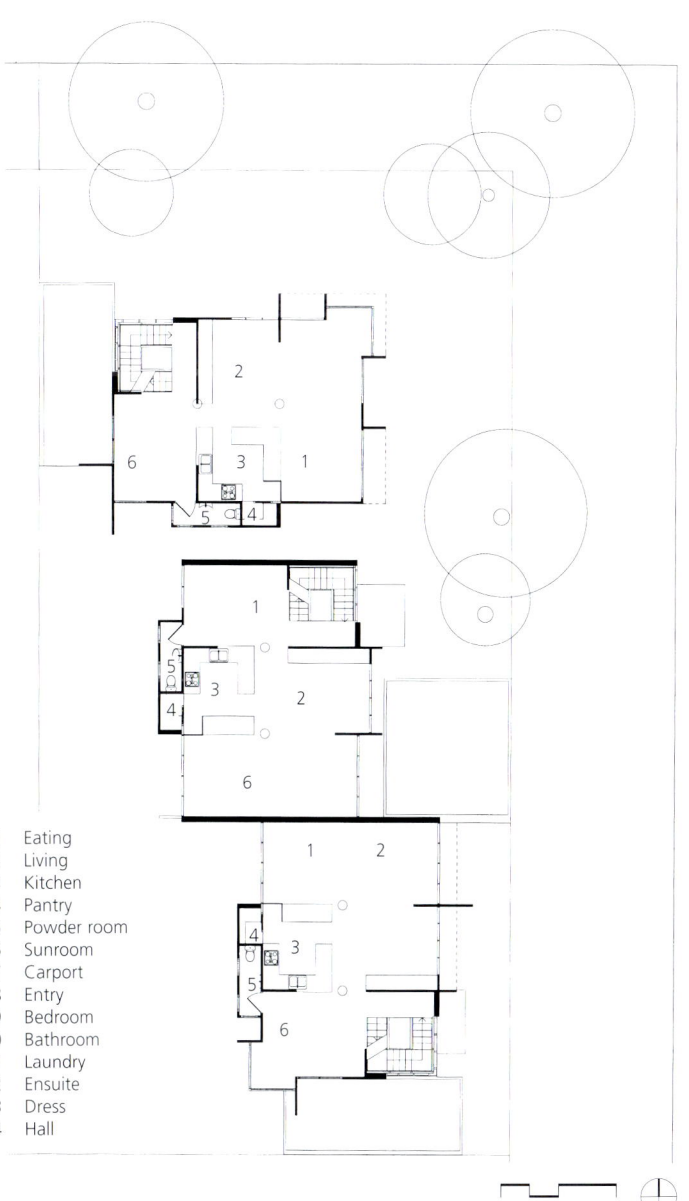

1 Eating
2 Living
3 Kitchen
4 Pantry
5 Powder room
6 Sunroom
7 Carport
8 Entry
9 Bedroom
10 Bathroom
11 Laundry
12 Ensuite
13 Dress
14 Hall

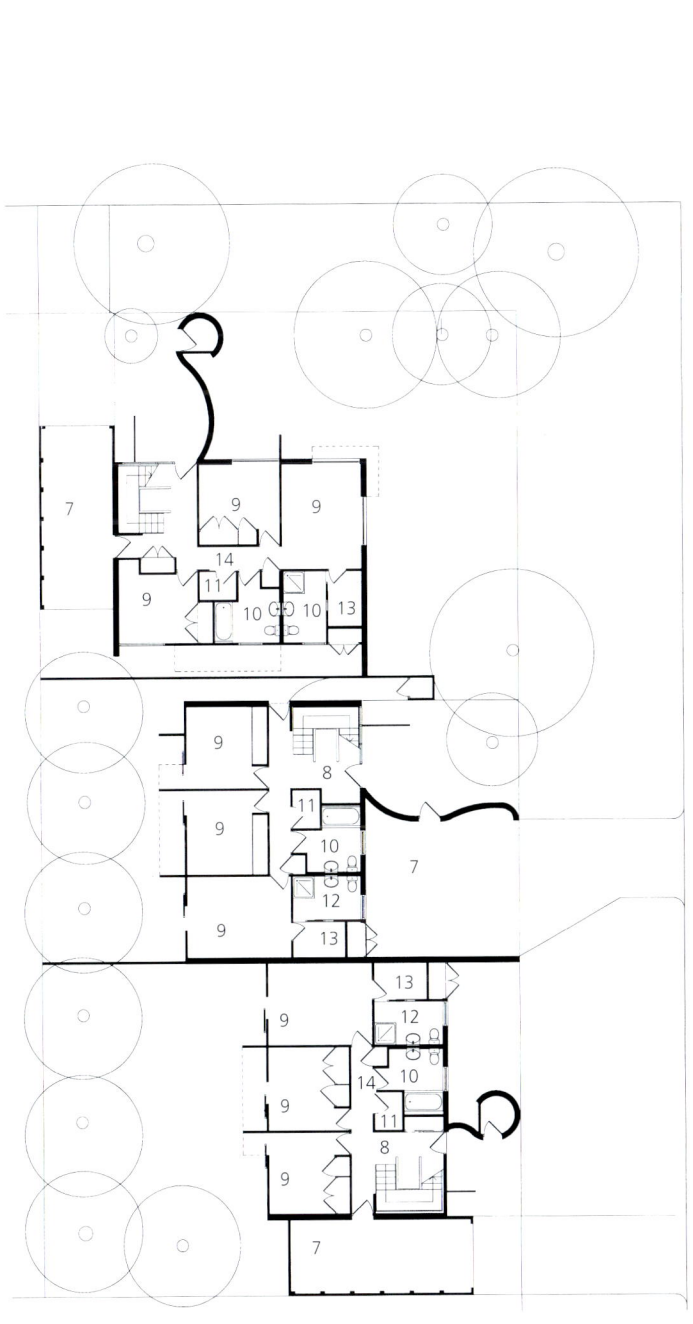

Great Escape
ROBERT CONTI ARCHITECT
Photography by Robert Conti

Not wanting to leave the convenience of the inner city for the suburbs, the owners of this beach house decided to build a weekender by the sea as a compromise. A holiday house with greater space would ideally supplement the limitations of their city townhouse.

A vacant site, overlooking the sea, was found an hour's drive from the city. When architect Robert Conti visited the site, he discovered the view of the sea was partially concealed by scrub. "I don't think they knew how fantastic the view really was. It was only after inspecting their neighbour's double-storey house that the spectacular vista became clear," he says. Conti's brief was to maximise the views and provide a sense of the outdoors.

The house doesn't pretend to camouflage itself but protrudes from its elevated site. "I react to the environment I'm working in, trying to pick up as many clues as possible," says Conti. The curved limestone wall that conceals the garage resembles a cliff face that has been hollowed out by the sea. The choice of limestone also compliments many of the limestone cottages that were originally built in the area. While it may be traditional to locate bedrooms above living areas, it was decided to reverse this design in order to capitalise on the views. Nevertheless, the four bedrooms downstairs are still orientated towards the sea and meet the client's brief for all rooms to have a view to the sea.

On the top level, the combined kitchen/living/dining area was designed with large glass sliding doors that directly open onto generous decking. The stainless-steel cables that enclose the exterior areas were chosen so as not to restrict the outlook. Even though the main living area appears generous in its dimensions, its size is deceptive. "I was slightly restricted by setback requirements and therefore decided to install upper windows to create the feeling of additional space." The curved roofline with its tiered window treatment literally draws your vision towards the sea. Protection, in the form of corrugated iron for the upper windows and a cedar-slatted pergola over the lower ones, means that the balcony can work as an additional room during the harsher summer months.

"The house looked like a hang-glider before it was completed. It was really quite beautiful in its skeletal form, touching the earth ever so slightly," says Conti.

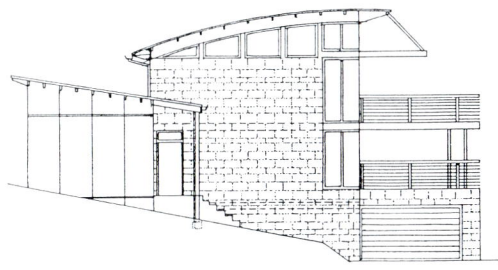
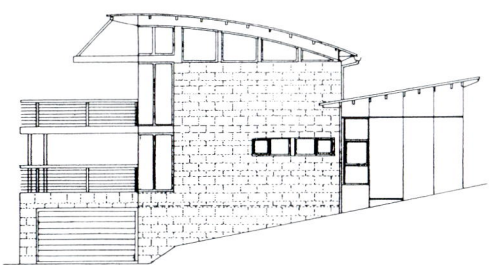

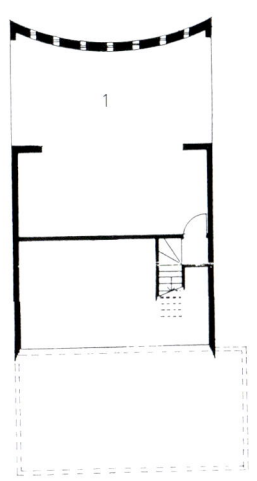
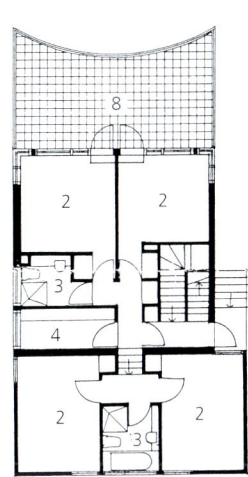
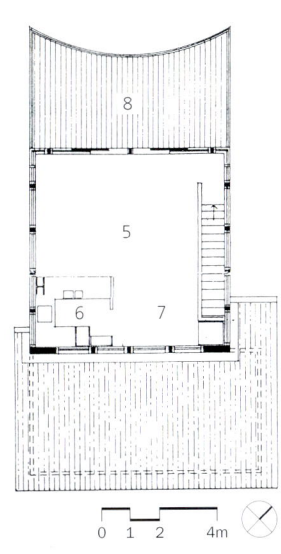

1 Garage
2 Bedroom
3 Bathroom
4 Laundry
5 Lounge
6 Kitchen
7 Dining
8 Balcony

0 1 2 4m

A Sense of Rhythm

UTZ-SANBY ARCHITECTS

Photography by Marian Riabic

While the water view vies for attention, so does this home's dramatic skillion roofline. Five angular roofs not only direct light into the interior, but also include, from every vantage point, views of the established eucalyptus trees. "Capturing these trees in the design was an important component to the brief," says architect Duncan Sanby of Utz–Sanby Architects who were commissioned to design this beachside house.

On a gradient of approximately 25 per cent, it was an ideal opportunity to design a two-storey home that could nestle into its bushland surrounds. Part of the brief also included designing two separate zones in the house, one for parents (the upper level), the other for their adult children and their children (the lower level). While designed as one house, the lower level is completely self-contained with a living, kitchen, dining and deck area, together with bedrooms. The upstairs level features a kitchen and living area. There are also two bedrooms, one for a guest. "The structural grid defines the parameters of the spaces within the house which are further reinforced by the roof form. The steel structure is set out in equal bays, which gives the house rhythm and order," says Sanby.

Though the configuration between the two levels differs significantly, generous protected deck areas feature on both floors. The main outdoor deck on the first level acts as the core of the house. Black mesh insect screens can be lowered on either side of the patio to allow the outdoor area to be used even during inclement weather. "The screen prevents insects from entering the house. When the screens are down, the house can be opened up entirely (with the large glass sliding doors)," says Sanby.

Keen to establish a view of the trees from every aspect, even the study, which is partially concealed by a bank of lacquered cupboards, was elevated to appreciate the environment. Sitting down behind the built-in desk also allows for some privacy. The open-plan house of approximately 300 square metres was also designed with good cross-ventilation. Louvred side windows and louvred highlight windows provide a continual breeze at most times of the day. "I think it's important for people to be able to change their environment, in a sense taking charge of the weather. The louvres and screens provide for exactly that," says Sanby. The angular roof design and the glazed walls in the home also create a transparency to the home. Because the materials used for this house are light; plywood, steel and glass, its impact on its surrounds is relatively minimal.

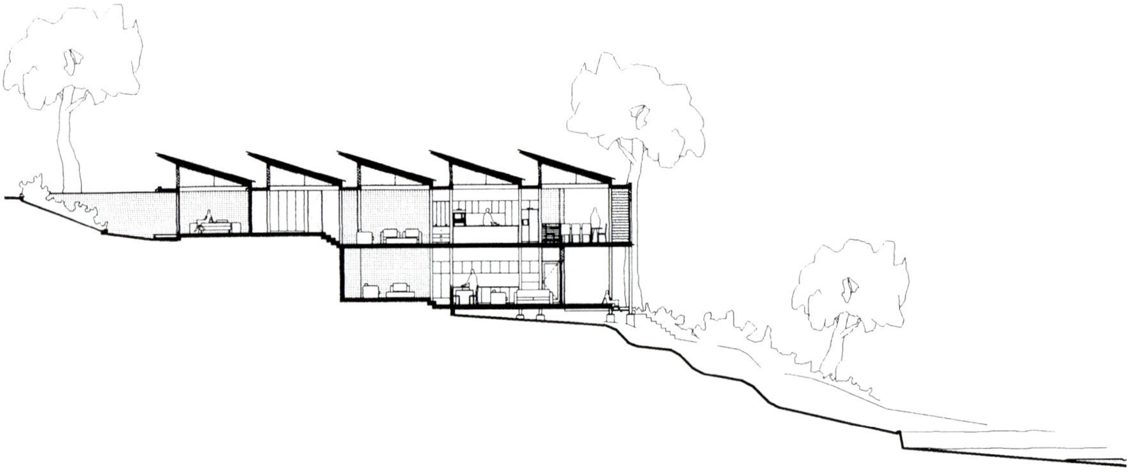

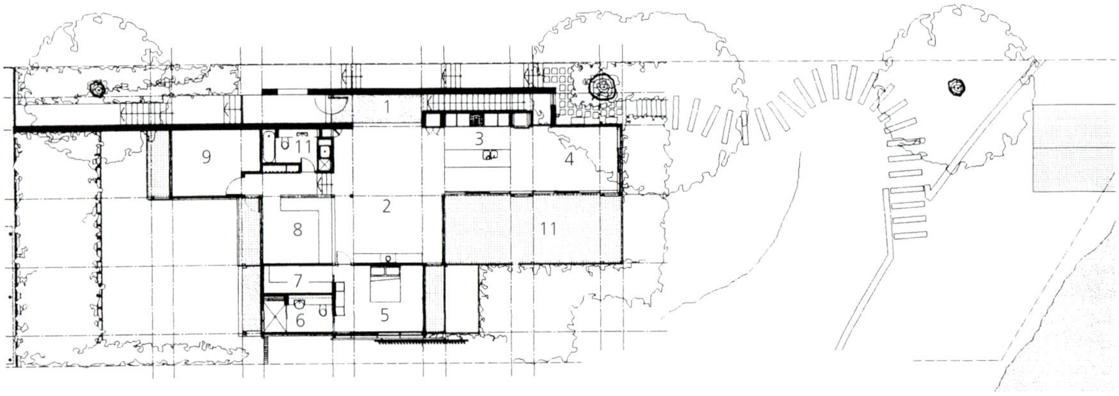

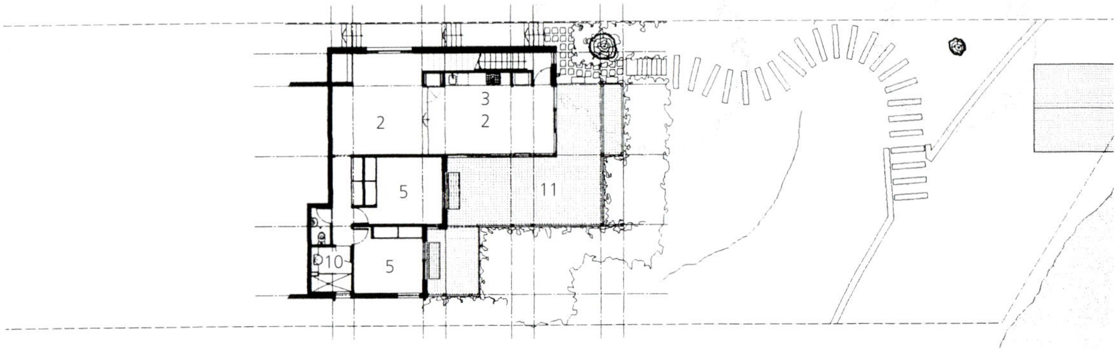

1	Entry
2	Living
3	Kitchen
4	Dining
5	Bedroom
6	Ensuite
7	Wardrobe
8	Study
9	Guestroom
10	Bathroom
11	Covered deck

Robust

JACKSON CLEMENTS BURROWS ARCHITECTS

Photography by Emma Cross of John Gollings Photography

Devoid of most coastal scrub, this beach house was elevated above the site to capture the distant views. The house had to be robust for a family with three children. "We saw this as an opportunity to explore the 'knock-about' qualities that a good beach house should embrace. Simplicity, a sense of fun and easily living," says architect Tim Jackson of the practice Jackson Clements Burrows, who designed the house.

The cue for this house came from the generic fibro beach shack. Like many of these homes, the cars, storage and games rooms are designed below and the open-plan living areas are above. To overcome a perceived dislocation between the ground floor and the first floor, a large earth mound was pushed up against the house. The mound, which is nestled under the verandah, anchors the house to the site. It also provides a soft landing for the children, jumping from the deck.

The house itself was sited partly as a response to the prevailing winds, with the bedroom wings acting as a shield. The protruding eaves also help to make the site less formidable. "The house is like a sectional extrusion which expands into the landscape. It's C-shaped," says Jackson. Materials were selected for their robust nature; a steel frame covered by corrugated iron and recycled timber cladding. In addition to steel poles, Jackson Clements Burrows used storage pods to anchor the house. "We were inspired by the vibrant-green seagrass beds of the area and the seaweed that grows up on the poles of the nearby jetty," says Jackson.

Unlike traditional beach shacks built in the 1950s, this design includes a void over the rumpus room (increasing the view over the coastal area and allowing for some parental supervision should it be required). Like the best beach houses, there is no concern when everyone returns from the beach with sand on their feet.

This house first appeared in Domain, in *The Age* newspaper.

DINING
LIVING
KITCHEN
VOID
BED 1
BATH 1
BATH 2
BED 2
BED 3
BED 4

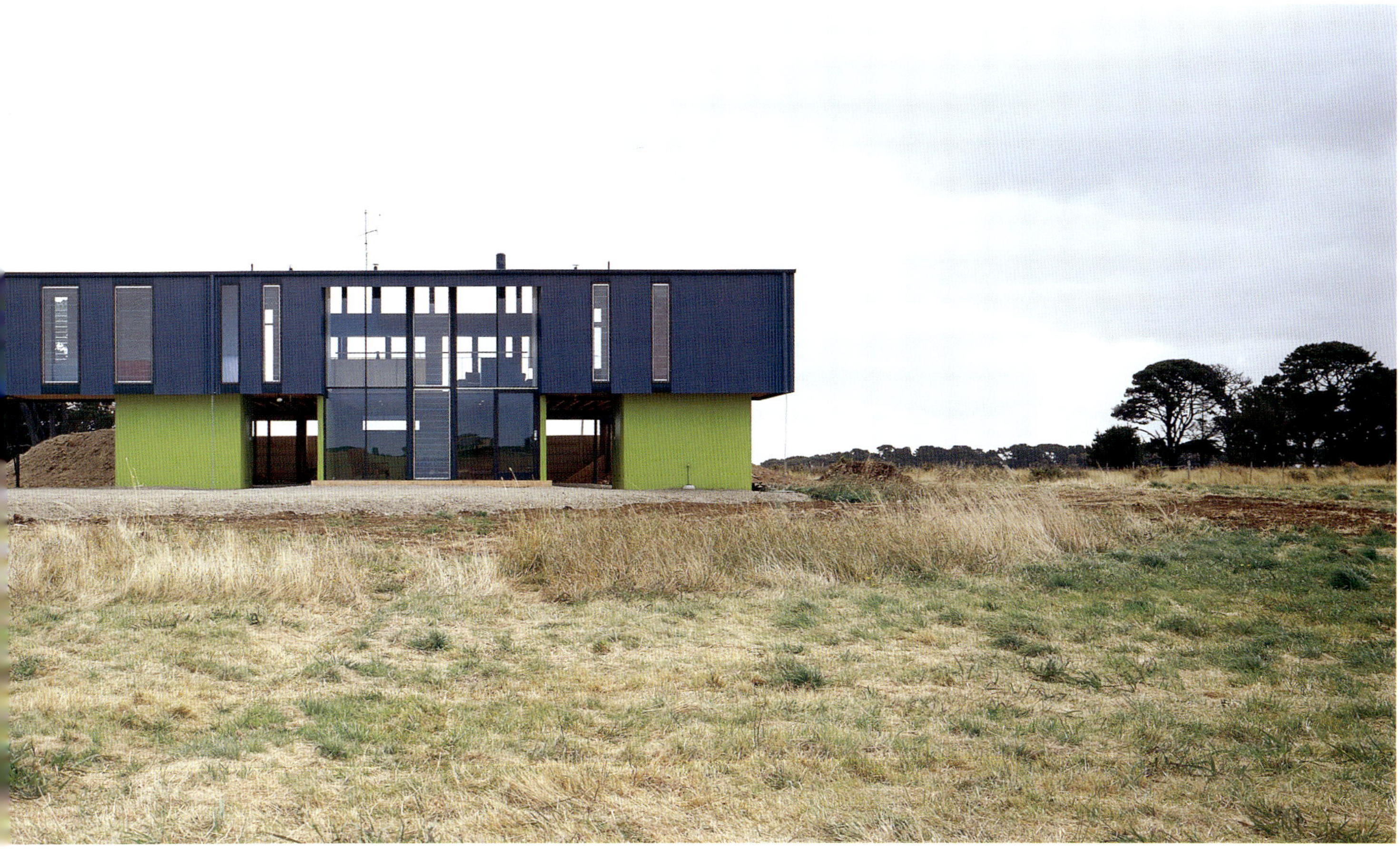

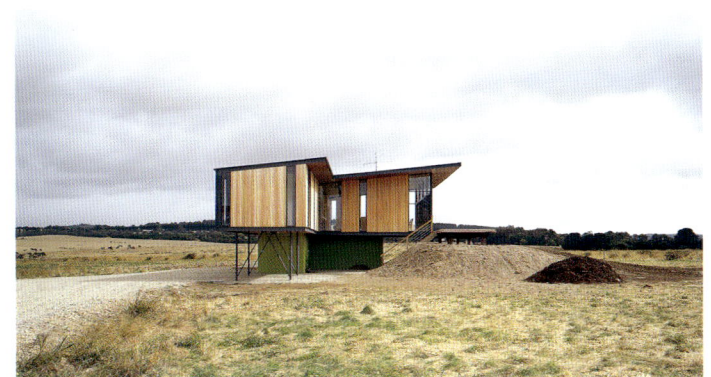

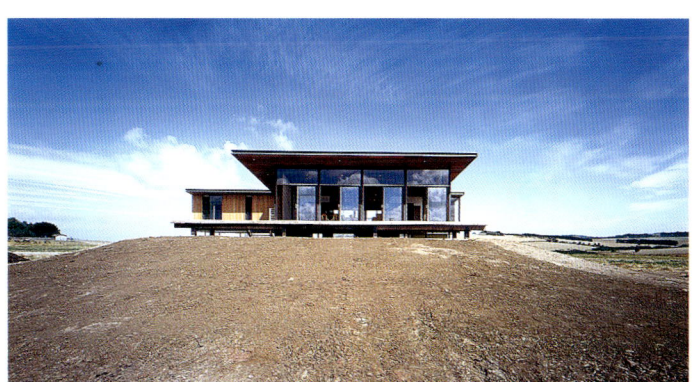

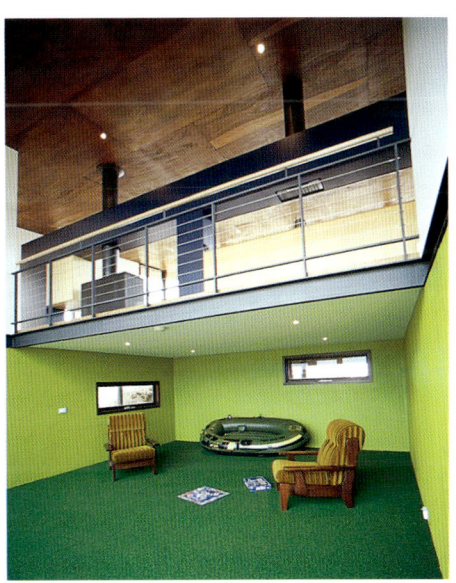

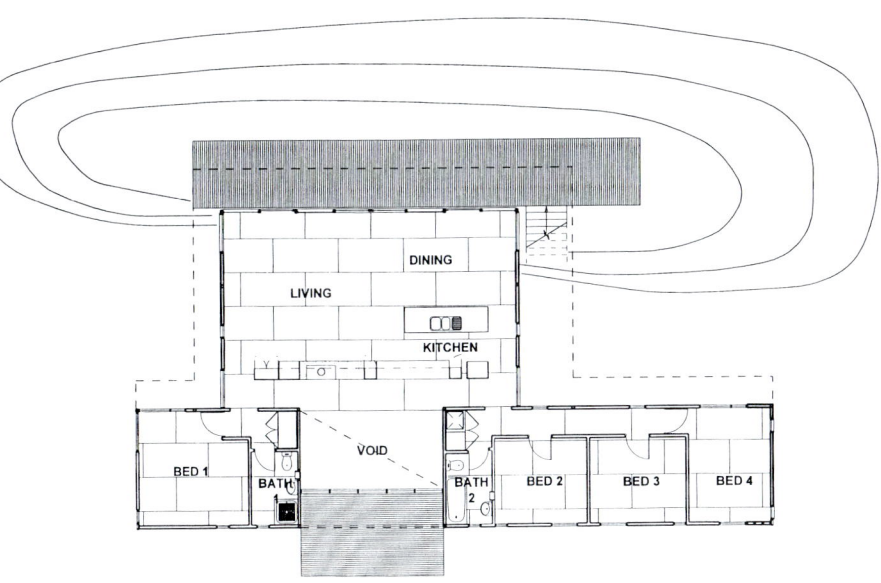

An Unexpected Space

ALLAN POWELL ARCHITECTS

Photography by Trevor Mein

Keen to design a house that had a sense of seclusion, architect Allan Powell designed this beach house circled by a massive sandstone wall. Framing the house on three sides, the sandstone wall forms a barrier to the neighbouring homes. "The idea came from an Italian village. It's similar to the space leftover between a cathedral and a city wall. The small unintentional space is then occupied by tables and chairs from the restaurant nearby," says Powell.

The house, overlooking a tennis court, is clearly zoned. On one side of the house are the children's three bedrooms and play area, while the other wing comprises the main bedroom and ensuite. Unifying the two zones, are the main kitchen, dining and living areas. While this division is typical of many of Powell's designs, the form and approach of the house is certainly unique.

Instead of the front door/entrance, being placed at the front of the site, Powell designed the house from a different angle. "The house is designed to drive down to the rear of the site and walk up to the front door via the side curved wall. It's only when you enter the kitchen and living area that you become aware of the expanse of the garden and the tennis court," says Powell. Using the edges of the site, rather than the traditional central position, meant Powell could retain the native vegetation, in particular the established cypress pines. "The curved walls also take in the changing moods of the moving sunlight," he adds.

There is a deliberate blurring in this house between the indoor and outdoor spaces. A concrete path leading to the front door continues through to the kitchen and living areas. "I'm not keen on the abrupt inside-out approach. I prefer using pergolas and filtering the light to create one space to explore. It was like creating a habitat against a wall," says Powell.

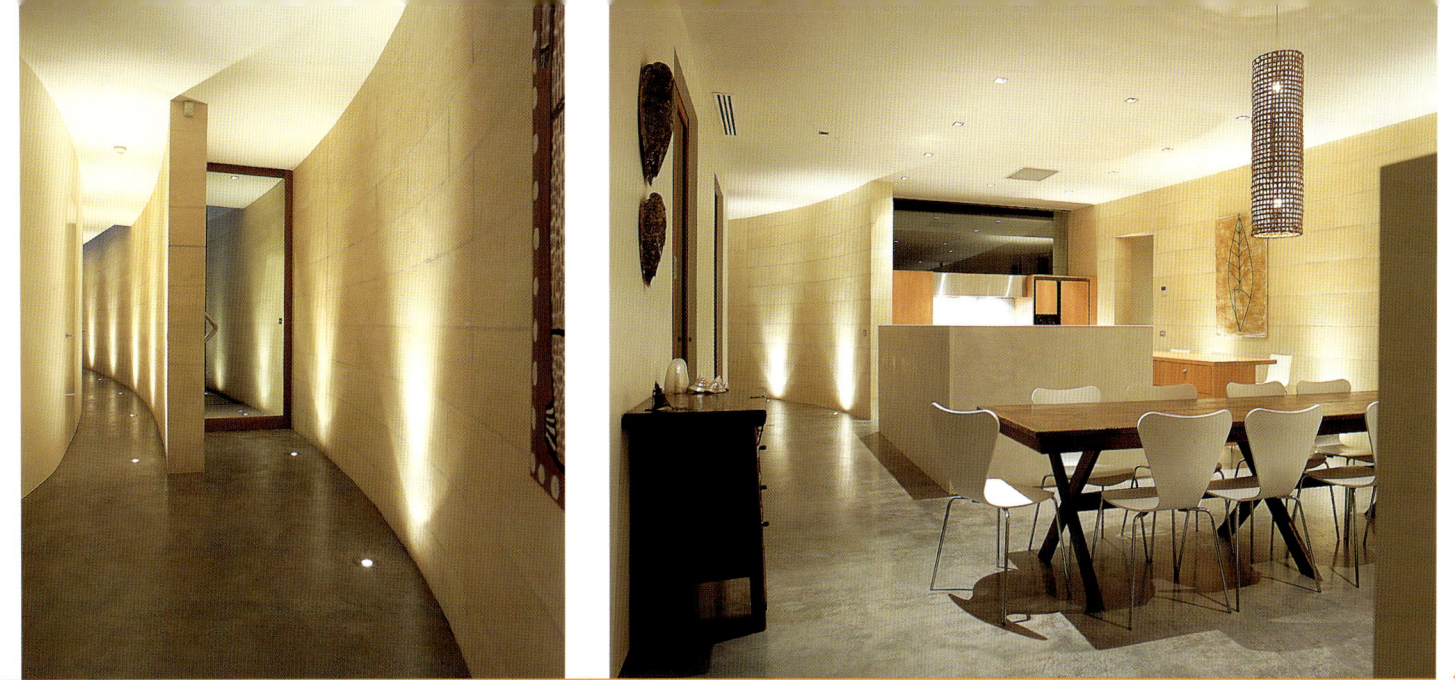

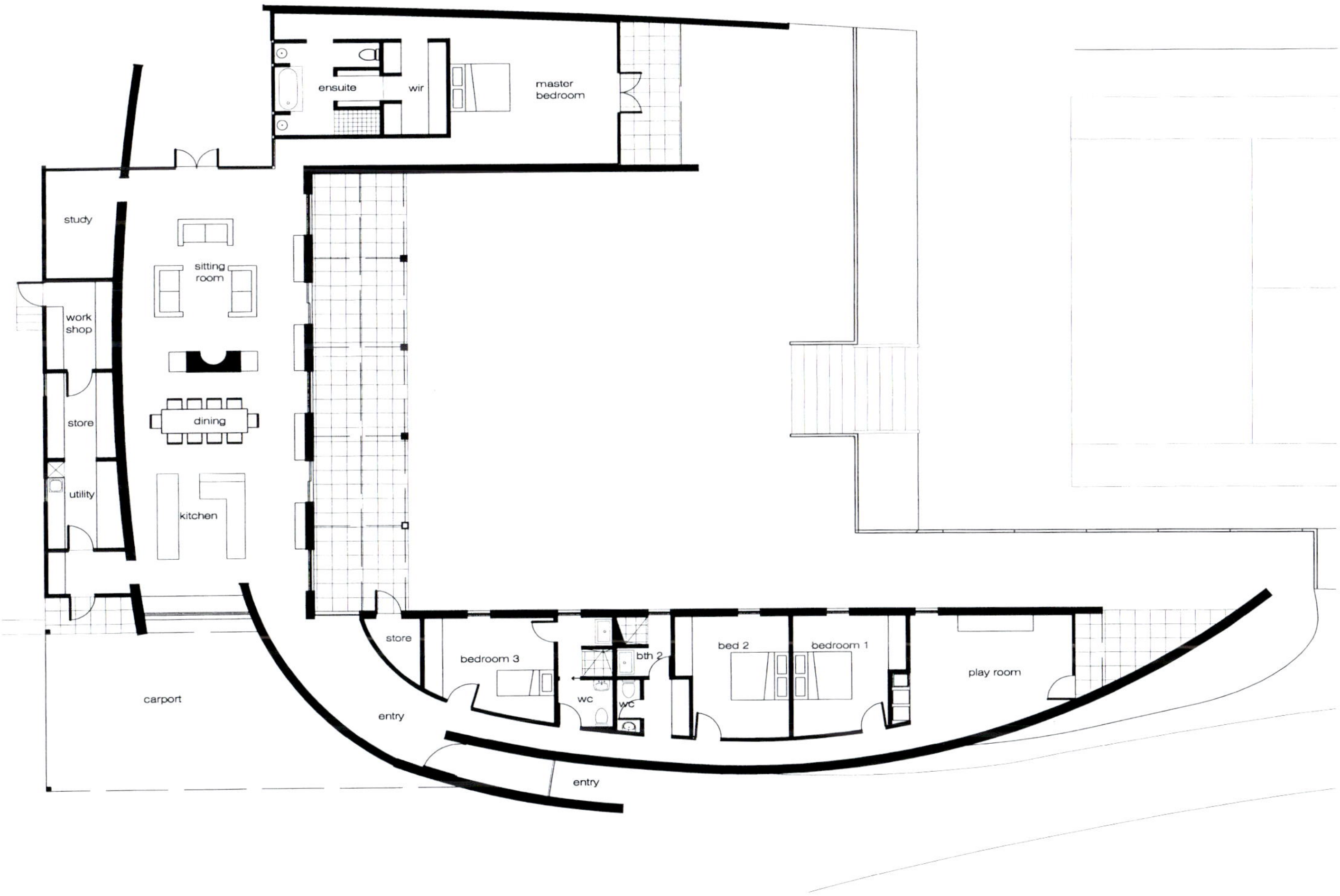
ensuite
wir
master bedroom
study
sitting room
work shop
store
dining
utility
kitchen
store
bedroom 3
bth 2
bed 2
bedroom 1
play room
wc
wc
carport
entry
entry

A Sustainable Approach

IREDALE PEDERSON HOOK ARCHITECTS

Photography by Adrian Lander and from the Office of Iredale Pederson Hook Architects

Designed by Iredale Pedersen Hook Architects, this house was created to cope with harsh extended summers. This striking house, made of BHP Colorbond, cantilevers over its coastal site, an hour's drive from the city.

Elevated on steel poles, the house's design was inspired by many of the surrounding homes, built in the 1960s. "We wanted to connect back to this period. It's also an appropriate way of building in an area of significant falls," says architect Adrian Iredale. This site, overlooking an estuary and mountain ranges, presented a 5-metre change in level. Instead of excavating the site, cutting, filling and redefining the landscape, the architects followed a more sustainable approach. "There's a bed of rock under the surface. Elevating the house not only minimised the impact of building on the site, but captured the views of the ranges," says Iredale.

By elevating the house, the architects created space below it. However, instead of the usual carport and storage solution, a series of verandahs were created. As the summers linger for months, the shaded verandahs act as secondary living areas, particularly at the height of the season. A native garden was also established under the house. "The platforms/decks are used for everything from barbeques to just relaxing. They're the coolest part of the house," says Iredale.

The large open-plan kitchen and living areas in the upper part of the house were designed for low-maintenance living. Large glass doors lead onto first-floor decks on either side of the living areas. And to ensure the front balcony is well protected, the home includes an angled façade. "The shape evokes the sixties. The canopy creates protection from the sun and the rain. It also adds to the privacy," says Iredale. While the finishes and materials of the interior were kept relatively simple, the architects devised a series of angled paint finishes for the interior walls. "Over a period of a day, the sun's rays move across the walls. The crossing of lines create a three-dimensional effect. The idea was to use the building as art," he says.

For the owners, this beach house is only a relatively short drive from where they live. But as soon as they arrive, there's an instant sense of relaxation. And even at the peak of summer, there are generous nooks under the house to explore.

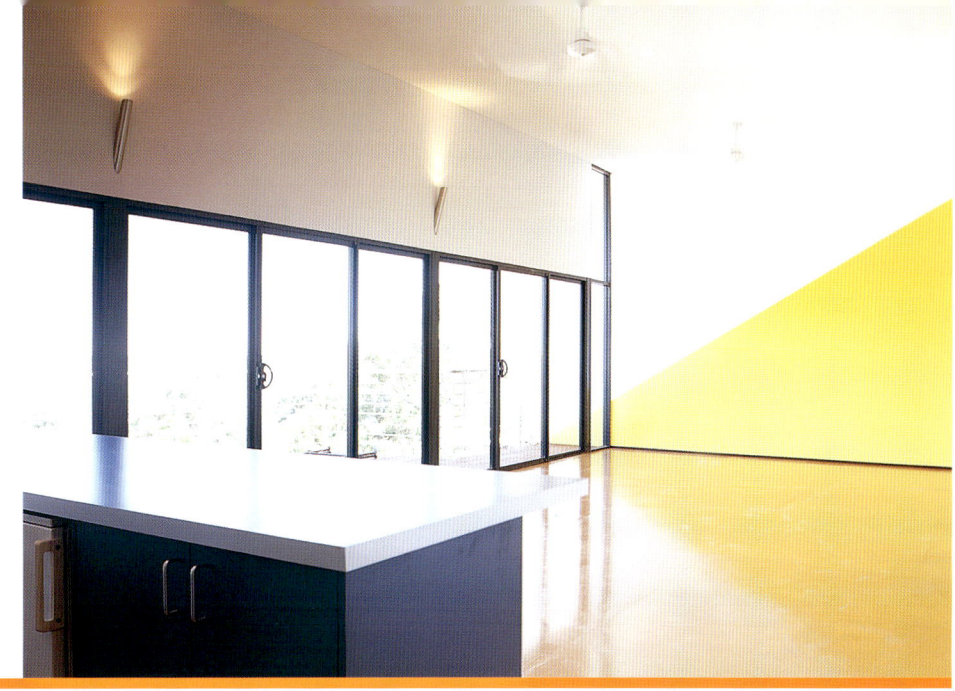

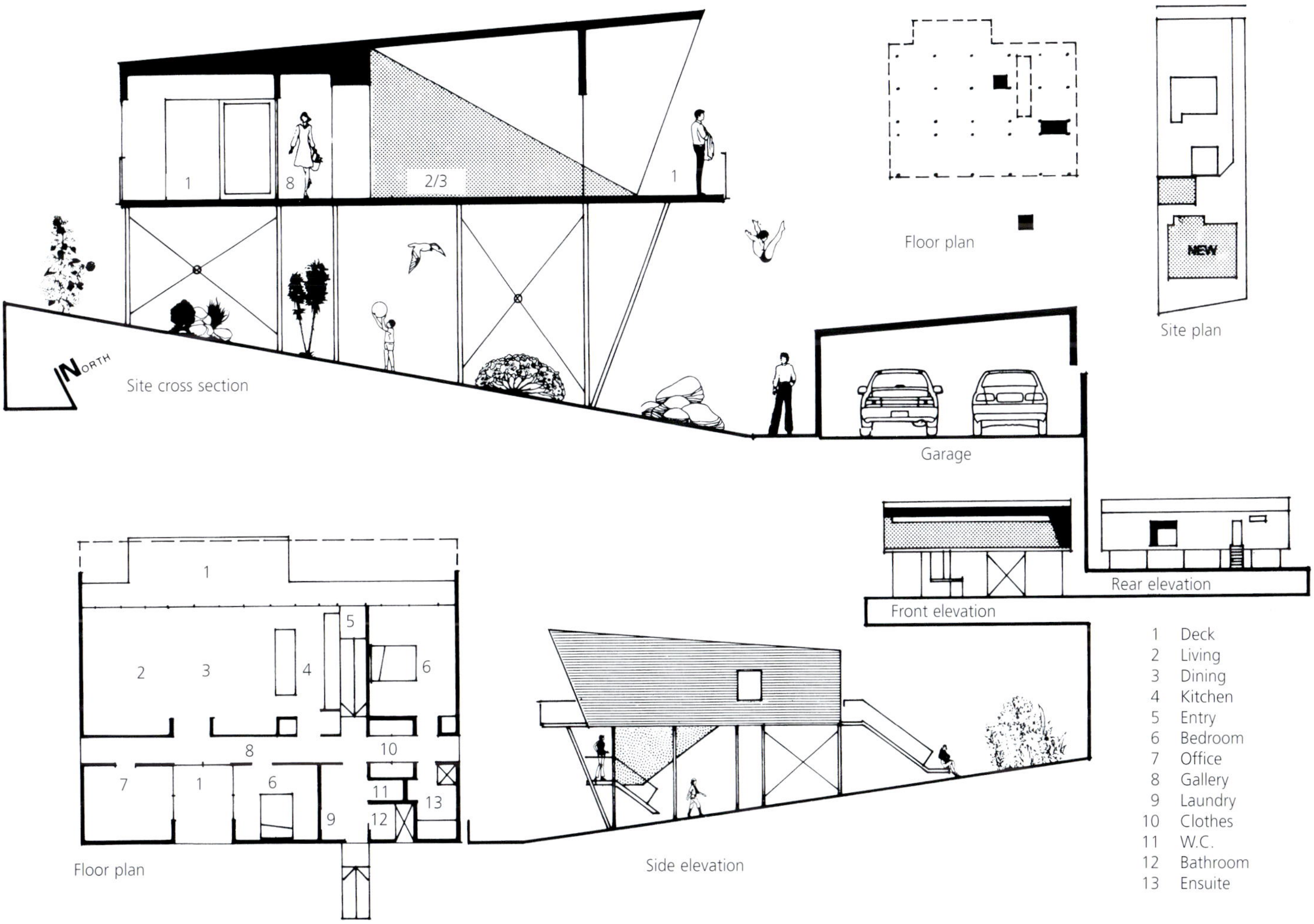
NORTH
Site cross section
1
8
2/3
1
Floor plan
NEW
Site plan
Garage
Front elevation
Rear elevation
Floor plan
1
2
3
4
5
6
7
1
6
8
9
10
11
12
13
Side elevation
1 Deck
2 Living
3 Dining
4 Kitchen
5 Entry
6 Bedroom
7 Office
8 Gallery
9 Laundry
10 Clothes
11 W.C.
12 Bathroom
13 Ensuite

A New Edge

NEIL & IDLE ARCHITECTS

Photography by Maikka Trupp

This beach house was originally a project home, one of many designed by architect Graeme Gunn in the 1970s. However, 30 years later, the square practical modernist box had lost its edge. Constructed in brick and timber on a concrete slab, the house was little more than 100 square metres.

Neil & Idle Architects were commissioned to give a more contemporary edge to this simple home, which is nestled into a coastal bushland setting. "It was simple, but it was in good condition. We didn't need to renovate the whole house," says architect Chris Idle. "We saw it in terms of simply threading a new element through the house," he adds.

The original bedrooms and bathroom were left intact. Only the kitchen and living areas required updating.

One of the problems with the original design was the ceiling height, measuring only 2.4 metres. "You could touch the timber beams with your hands," says Idle. To overcome this problem, the ceiling was lifted and the living room was extended to form one open kitchen and living area. The extension of the new roof was constructed with a fibro-cement corrugated sheet. Painted in grape colour, the rippled façade echoes many traditional beach shacks in the area. "It also reduces the summer heat," says Idle. "We installed large glass sliding doors to the deck. We didn't want to create a glass box that would be difficult to live in. We also wanted to frame the views," he adds.

The original kitchen was in one corner of the house. Too small to be of use to the current owners, the architects designed an entirely new kitchen. A laminated veneer central island bench now cantilevers into the new entry which features polished concrete floors. To further accentuate and define the living areas in the open-plan arrangement, timber floors were slightly elevated.

While the house appears significantly larger than before, the floor area was only increased from 100 to 120 square meters. The owners can now enjoy the leafy coastal surrounds through their new glass windows or from the tiered decks gently cascading over the site.

1 Master bedroom
2 Bedroom
3 Bathroom
4 W.C.
5 Laundry
6 Outdoor shower
7 Kitchen
8 Living
9 Entry

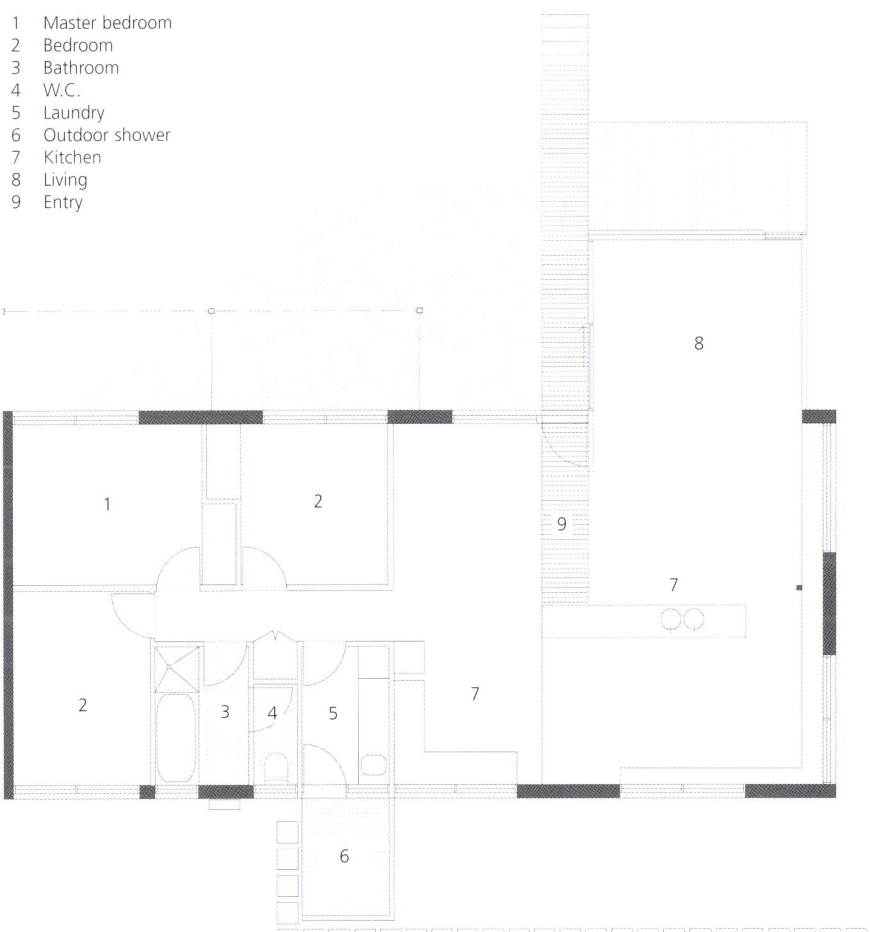

A Sense of Enclosure

RANDLES HILL STRAATVEIT ARCHITECTS

Photography by Richard Glover

Designed by architects Peter Hill and Brendan Randles of Randles Hill Straatveit Architects, this beach house looks over a rocky surf beach. On the other side of the headland, a five-minute walk, are more protected beaches.

Located at the end of a cul-de-sac, the recent subdivision is dotted with suburban-style housing. On a fairly small site of approximately 400 square metres, the clear and uninterrupted view of the water was the main attraction. For the owners, who live in the city, the four-hour drive to this location offered an affordable entry into this idyllic environment. The clients wanted a low-budget weekender that would not resemble their more suburban neighbours. "They didn't want the house to look like a project home or be open to passers-by. They wanted the sea to be the focus," says architect Peter Hill.

While the beaches past the headland are protected, the beach directly in front of this house is windswept and exposed. As the owners have friends in the vicinity, they knew the importance of sheltered outdoor areas. "Their friends had to do some serious planting to create a barrier against the wind. They knew that an open deck simply wasn't going to be used, however attractive the views were going to be," says Hill.

The architects designed a very simple weekender, only 110 square metres in size. The V-shaped house consists of the main living area, dining and kitchen to one side of the entrance. The other side consists of the main bedroom. And above the bathroom (at the point of the V) is a small loft space. Effectively one open-plan space, the loft acts as a viewing platform to the spaces below. Used as a space for guests or alternatively a home office, the loft features an exposed hardwood rafter and hoop pine-lined ceilings.

Materials have been kept simple, bagged brickwork on the exterior and rendered brickwork on the interior. Even the chimney and open fireplace is rendered brick. "We wanted to keep the materials consistent and not detract from the view," says Hill.

V-shaped walls create a protective nook on one side of the house. And outside the main bedroom and main living area, the architects extended the walls for protection against the wind. In the dining area, conceived of as a sheltered box, there is a long slit window at waist height. "When you're sitting down at the table, you can still enjoy the views to the water," he adds.

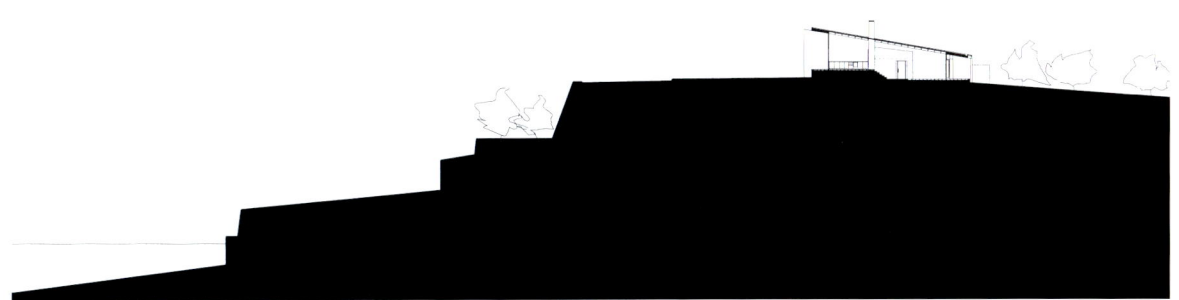

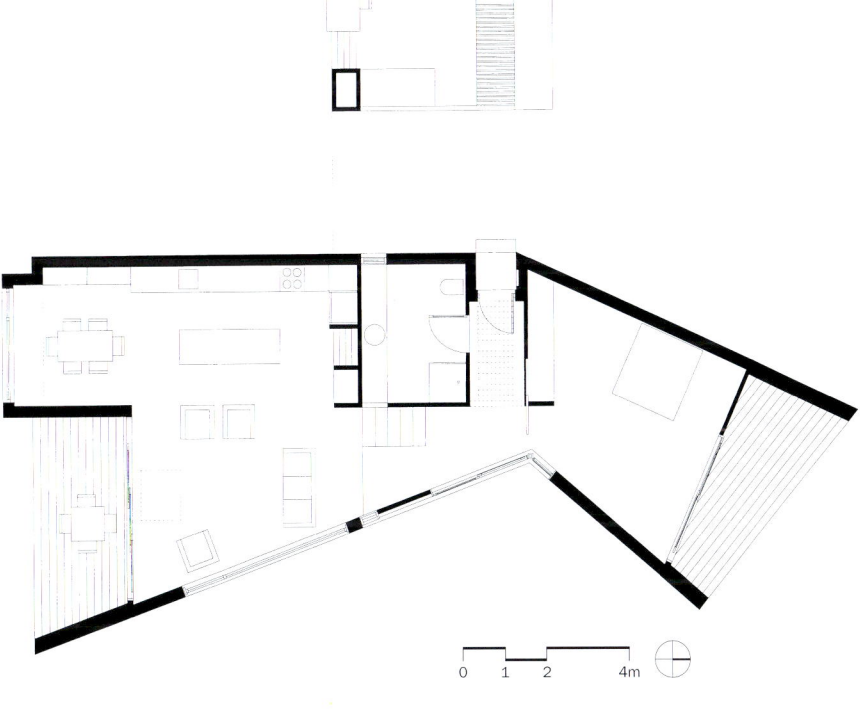

A Horizontal Band

DALE JONES-EVANS ARCHITECTS

Photography by Trevor Mein

Designed in a horizontal band across the site, this beach house is a mere 6 metres in width. Its length is considerably greater at 16 metres. "My client wanted to include a tennis court on the site. By the time we made all the allowances (including landscaping and the required setback from the road), the site was considerably reduced," says architect Dale Jones-Evans who designed the house.

However, these constraints weren't going to undermine the strength of the design. Dale Jones-Evans drew inspiration from the ocean and the strong horizon lines enhancing the site. Elevated above the landscape, the two-storey beach house consists of a small glass entry (laundry and solarium) with the bedrooms, kitchen and living areas above. "The see-through under-space allows a seamless reading of the site, the surrounding land, cliff edges and seascape, while the floating bunker elevates the living spaces to the views. I wanted the whole to be clearly read," says Jones-Evans. The view of the sea and the scrub from the tennis court are both clear from the elongated band of windows in the living area. The windows in the living room itself are set at 'eyebrow' level. "They're more similar to a camera aperture, which carefully frames the view, rather than a window specifically designed for natural light (although the sunlight entering the house is generous)," he says.

The same sense of transparency is evident in the kitchen. Framed by two symmetrical outdoor decks either side (overlooking the tennis court) and large sliding glass doors, the division between the indoor and outdoor spaces is deliberately blurred. When the glass doors are left open the outdoor space appears to be contained in the building. "It replaces the notion of the verandah."

The house sits on a raw galvanised-steel platform creating two undercrofts at either end for the parking of cars. The undercrofts also create outdoor areas, cool and protected from the summer sunlight. The material language of the building is direct – concrete, steel, glass, timber and compressed cement-sheet cladding. "The materials are a play on the 1950s beach shack. This house is also quite raw. It has a weathered feeling, almost like a piece of driftwood," Jones-Evans says.

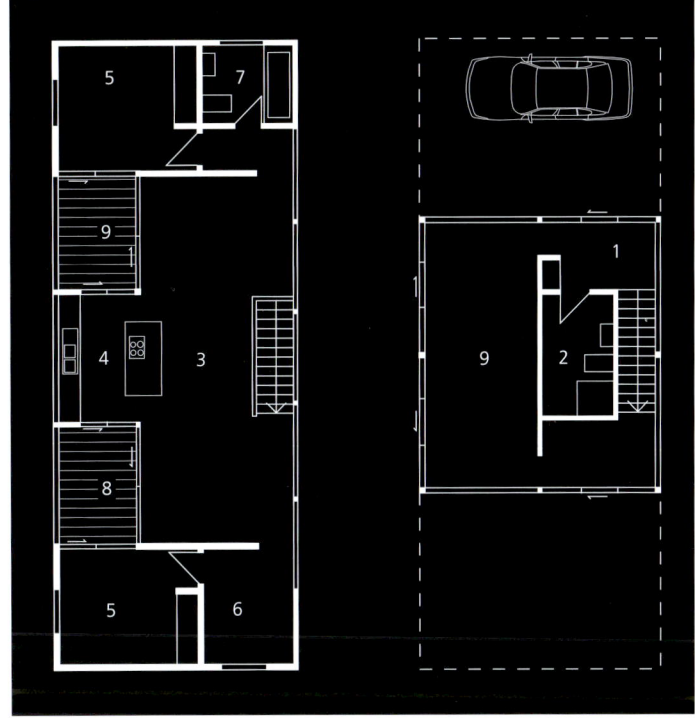

1	Entry	6	Study
2	Laundry	7	Bathroom
3	Living/dining	8	Deck
4	Kitchen	9	Solarium
5	Bedroom		

A Journey
STEPHEN JOLSON ARCHITECT
Photography by Scott Newett

Designed by the office of Stephen Jolson Architect, this house is located above a golf course. While the course attracts golfers from around the world, so does the area's rugged coastline.

The 270-degree views over the golf course and surf are sensational, but so is the strength of the prevailing winds. With the inclement climate, it is understandable that the clients were keen on a concrete house. "They wanted a solid home and had always wanted to live in a house totally made of concrete," says architect Stephen Jolson, who designed the house with Adam Muggelton and Bianca Winter. Designed for a couple and their extended family, the 400-square-metre house (excluding garages and terraces) is divided into two wings, separated by a concrete catwalk or drawbridge.

On one side of the house are the main bedroom, kitchen and living area. The other wing accommodates the other bedrooms (including guests) and the study. "Our clients didn't want to feel as if they were occupying a large rambling house if they decided to come down and stay on their own," says Jolson.

There are three distinct views of this precast concrete house. From the road, the house appears as a monolith, which has erupted from the ground. The raw exposed concrete follows the curves of the road. But through the front door, the house starts to reveal itself as the first part of a journey. "From the catwalk, the ocean appears to be a calm element. It's only when you descend into the living areas that you start to appreciate the full strength of the ocean and the ferocity of the waves," says Jolson.

Designed over one level (with the exception of the garage), the form of the house is clearly outlined with horizontal floor and roof plates both constructed in galvanised post-form channels. Thick vertical precast concrete panels create a strong juxtaposition in the design. "The house was designed as a viewing platform," says Jolson.

And while the views are impressive, the architects were also mindful of the ever-changing weather patterns. A large outdoor deck was inserted on the more protected side of the site.

For the interior, bamboo was used extensively, from the floors to the joinery. "Bamboo is incredibly strong, there's no movement in bamboo and it's particularly refined," says Jolson, who also used bamboo to create a datum line across the living room wall. "It mimics the horizon line of the ocean," he adds.

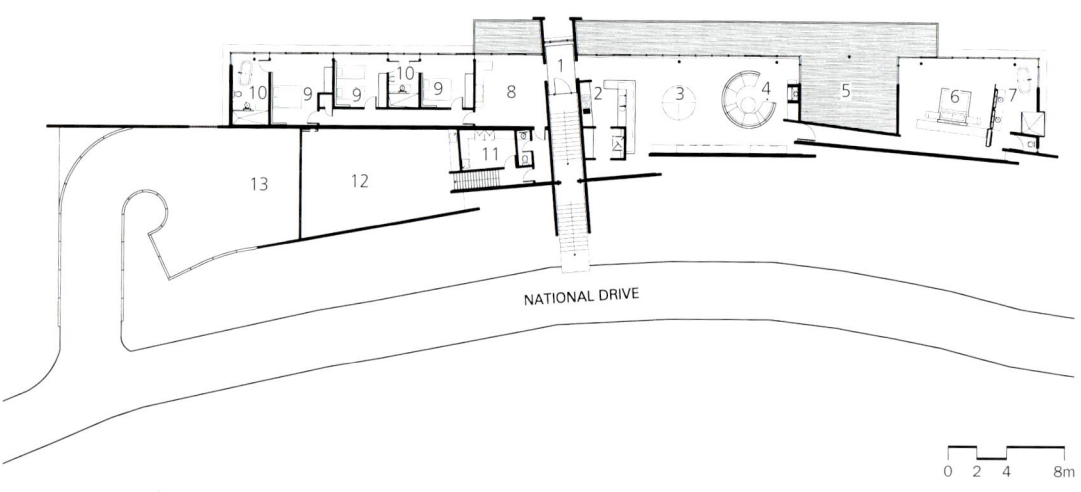

1	Entry
2	Kitchen
3	Meals
4	Lounge
5	Courtyard
6	Master bedroom
7	Ensuite
8	Study
9	Guest bedroom
10	Guest bathroom
11	Laundry
12	Carport
13	Driveway

Through the Back Door

CRAIG ROSSETTI ARCHITECT

Photography by Andrew Ashton and by Tim Griffith

Designed by architect Craig Rossetti, this intriguing house is located at the end of a long winding road. Set on 50 acres of windswept land, dense kerb-side planting around the house adds to the sense of arrival.

Unlike some beachside houses, which feature endless rooms, this house is relatively modest in scale, given the number of occupants. Designed for a family with four children, the house features only two bedrooms, one for the parents and the other for the children. "They (the children) all bunk in together. There are two trundle beds," says Rossetti. While the brief included two bedrooms and a separate kitchen and living area, the architect's design brief was relatively open. "They said they wanted it to feel like a farm house," he says.

Like a farmhouse, which is often entered through the back door, Rossetti designed the two bedrooms (separated by a bathroom) closest to the front door. The approach to the living area therefore becomes a journey, where the views to the sea in the distance are not immediately revealed. The materials used for the house also evoke a rural ambience. The ceilings are made of straw and the walls are made of concrete and rusting steel.

The shape of the house, a subtle curve, follows the contours of the land. Nestled into a knoll, the architect was mindful of the prevailing winds and the need to set up the views. The curvaceous spine wall, made of concrete, creates a gradual appreciation of the site. Concrete-rendered blade walls, directed towards the pool, intensify each outlook. "The blades also reduce the amount of sun entering the house," says Rossetti.

The central deck/patio area between the two wings (sleeping and living) is the most protected outdoor area. The internal spaces spill over into the deck area, with the kitchen's concrete bench extending into the courtyard (with built-in barbeque) to create alfresco dining. "It's not about the containment of space. The idea is to explore the landscape," says Rossetti.

While the house appears relatively simple (although in reality a far more complex design), it took the architect a couple of years to submit the plans. "My clients were travelling endlessly. The designs were sent by fax. My clients often paced motel rooms to compare the dimensions," says Rossetti, who has noticed that their travelling time has been considerably reduced since the beach house was completed.

This house first appeared in Domain, in *The Age* newspaper.

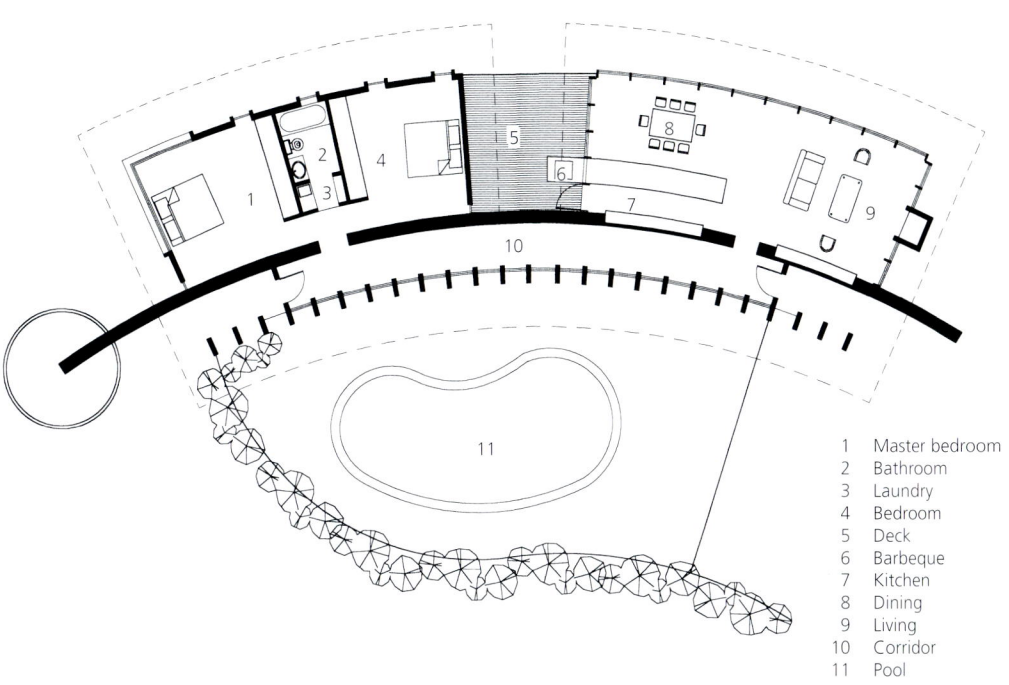

1 Master bedroom
2 Bathroom
3 Laundry
4 Bedroom
5 Deck
6 Barbeque
7 Kitchen
8 Dining
9 Living
10 Corridor
11 Pool

Strategic Incisions

BREARLEY MIDDLETON ARCHITECTS

Photography by Erica Lauthier

The original 1950s brick home was quite comfortable. It had three bedrooms and even an ensuite. However, when architect James Brearley of Brearley Middleton Architects inspected the house, he could see that it wasn't large enough for what the owners wanted. But he didn't think it warranted total demolition either.

The architects decided to retain the existing 1950s house and add a second storey, which would allow for larger and more adventurous spaces. With a view of the cliffs and the ocean ahead, the brief emphasised the importance of capturing the 360-degree views. "We wanted to watch the sun rise and set. We weren't interested in looking at paintings on a wall or vases of flowers," says the owner. Rather than designing traditional-shaped windows that frame the view, Brearley Middleton designed a ribbon of windows of different proportions around the whole house. "The windows are a hybrid form which allow you to see the views from a number of angles," says Brearley.

An important influence on the design came from the American artist Gordon Matta-Clarke, who is renowned for inserting cuttings into a building. Like the strategic incisions that Matta-Clarke applied, there are a series of planes that allow for a cross section of views throughout the house. There are fewer rooms on the upper level, a kitchen and deck, a dining and living room, together with the one main bedroom. The living room, with its grape-coloured ceiling, walls and carpet, appears to have been carved out of the volume. The walls, which are 700 millimetres wide in part, include built-in day beds. In contrast, the dining room appears quite skeletal, with its plywood walls and recycled timber rafters.

In contrast to the subdued living areas, the panoramic views illuminate the internal spaces. "We wanted to heighten the different activities within the house and it required a number of treatments rather than one approach," Brearley says.

Even though the number of people staying in the house can vary from two to 10, depending on the number of children and friends that stay over, finding a place to sleep isn't difficult. If a bed can't be found downstairs, the day beds surrounding the living room become instant accommodation.

This house first appeared in Domain, in *The Age* newspaper.

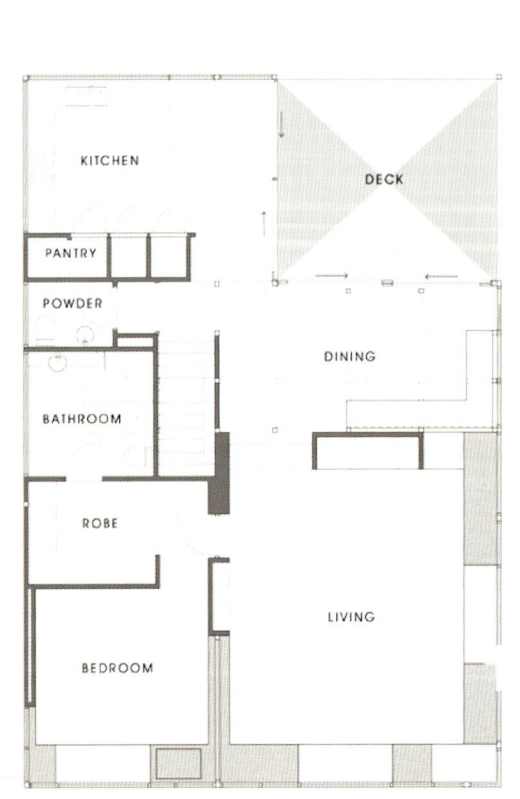

On a Crest
JOHN WARDLE ARCHITECTS
Photography by John Gollings

Located on the crest of a hill, a short walk from the shore, this beach house was designed to take in the ocean views. Designed by architect John Wardle, the house is as breathtaking as the views.

This large timber-lined home, featuring stonewalls and zinc cladding, is organised over two levels. On the lower level are three bedrooms for the children, a bathroom and play area, together with garage and laundry facilities. On the upper floor are the main bedroom, dressing area and ensuite, study, living, kitchen and dining area. And wherever one stands in the house, there's a water-view. A shallow pebbled moat frames the entrance (with a drawbridge) and a swimming pool is adjacent to the main living area. The house has generous living spaces and a separate wing for children and guests – the latter is embedded into the hill that supports the elevated living platform above. The result is a house that presents as a finely crafted timber box, floating above a rendered base. "We used a palette of natural materials, locally sourced where possible, to integrate the house with its natural setting," says Wardle.

Entry to the house is via a stone wall. The wall not only provides privacy from neighbouring homes, but also protects the house from hot summer winds. Once inside, the living spaces open out through expansive windows and glazed doors to the valley and ocean below. Sliding and pivotal screens in the living areas offer additional privacy and also control the amount of sunlight entering the spaces. "The house is designed to be responsive to the natural elements and can be finely tuned by adjusting the various blind systems, external sliding doors and ventilation panels to suit the prevailing weather conditions," says Wardle.

The house is planned around a central hearth, which acts as a focus for the living and dining spaces. All the spaces on the upper level are visually linked with a floating plywood ceiling system. The form of the house is a simple skillion that reflects the interior volume. There are three main elements on the site, the protective high stone garden walls and rendered block work, the skillion house form leaning against the walls and the swimming pool pod. "The planning of the house reflects a recurring theme in our work, a preference to extrude space along the longitudinal axis," says Wardle.

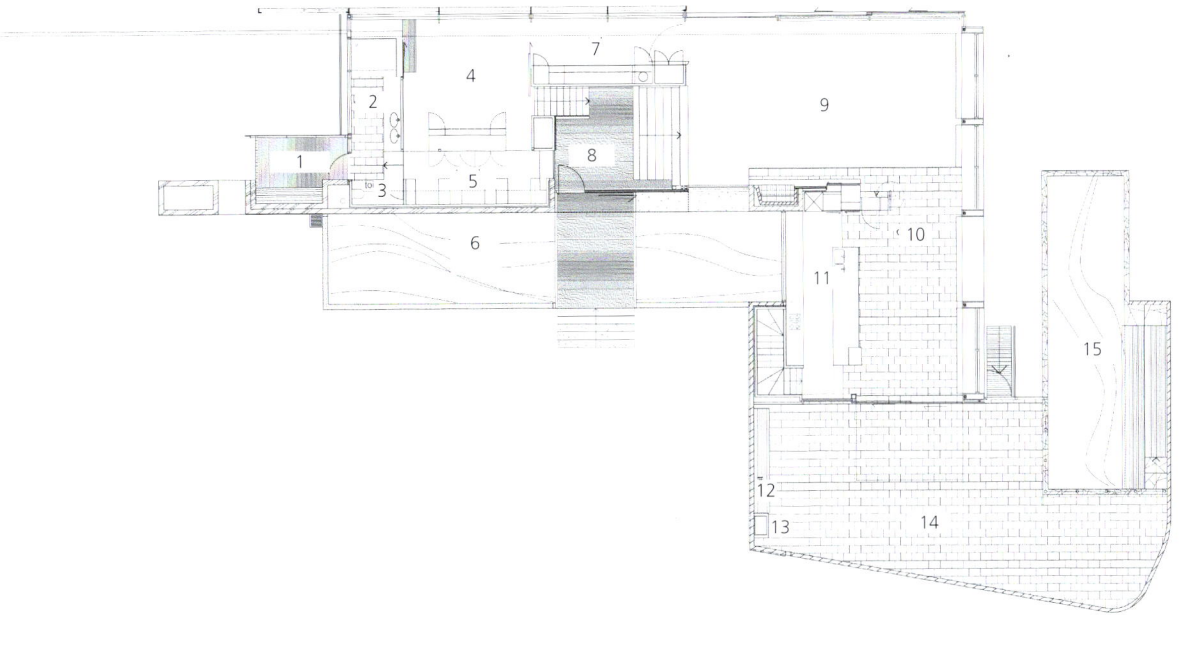

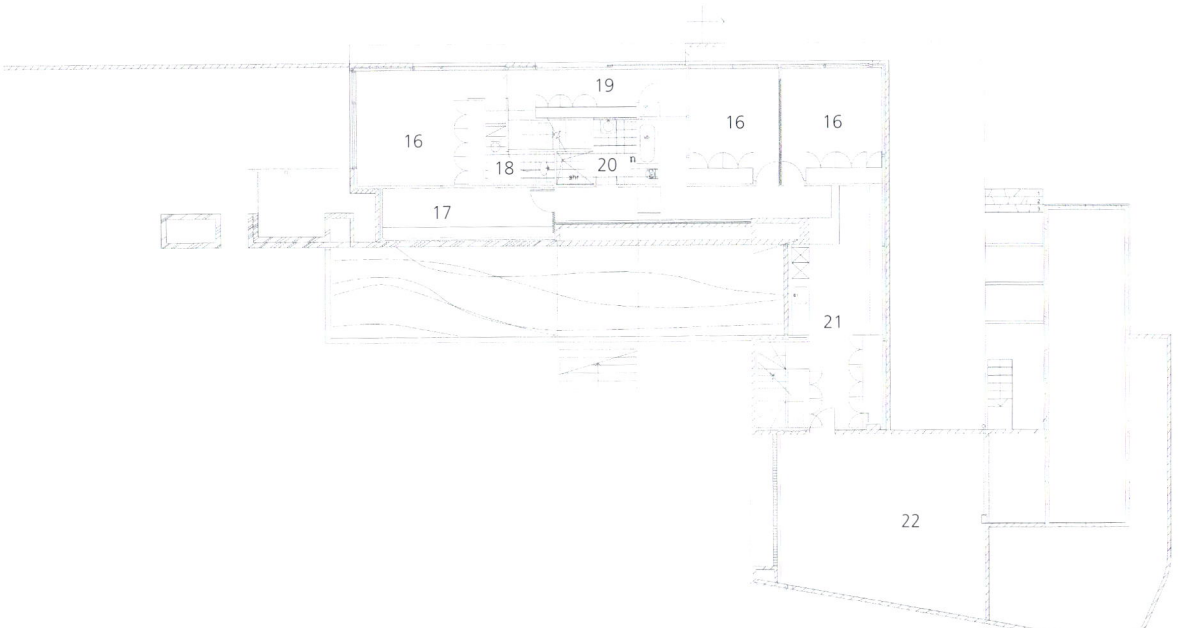

1. Balcony
2. Ensuite
3. W.C.
4. Main bedroom
5. Dressing room
6. Seasonal pebble pool
7. Study
8. Entry
9. Living
10. Dining
11. Kitchen
12. Seat
13. Barbeque
14. Terrace
15. Swimming Pool
16. Bedroom
17. Cellar
18. Powder room
19. Playroom
20. Bathroom
21. Laundry and store
22. Garage

FEATURED ARCHITECTS

Architects

ALLAN POWELL ARCHITECTS
19 Victoria Street,
St Kilda, Vic 3182
Phone: +(61) 3 9534 8367
Fax: +(61) 3 9525 3615
Email: allan@allanpowell.com.au
Page 158

COL BANDY ARCHITECTS
4 Upton Road,
Windsor, Vic 3182
Phone: +(61) 3 9529 8722
Fax: +(61) 3 9529 7917
Email: colbandy@mira.net
Page 124

ARCHITECTS INK
265 The Parade,
Beulah Park, SA 5067
Phone: +(61) 8 8364 1434
Fax: +(61) 8 8364 0098
Email: adelaide@architectsink.com.au
Page 140

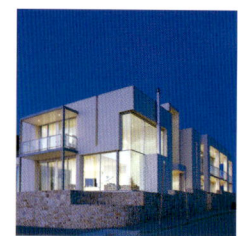

CON BASTIRAS ARCHITECT
13 Valmai Avenue,
Kings Park, SA 5034
Phone: +(61) 8 8271 3469
Fax: +(61) 8 8271 0712
Email: bastiras@senet.com.au
Page 50

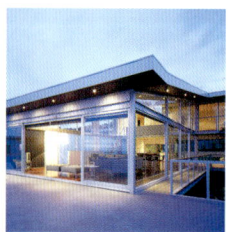

BBP ARCHITECTS
93 Kerr Street,
Fitzroy, Vic 3065
Phone: +(61) 3 9416 1486
Fax: +(61) 3 9416 1438
Email: info@bbparchitects.com
Page 56

CONNOR + SOLOMON ARCHITECTS
61 Darling Street,
Balmain, NSW 2041
Phone: +(61) 2 9810 1329
Fax: +(61) 2 9810 4109
Email: avs@coso.com.au
Page 118

BREARLEY MIDDLETON ARCHITECTS
Level 2/358, Lonsdale Street,
Melbourne, Vic 3000
Phone: +(61) 3 9642 5115
Fax: +(61) 3 9642 5114
Email: archi@brearley.net.au
Page 180

CRAIG ROSSETTI ARCHITECT
28 Gwynne Street,
Richmond, Vic 3121
Phone: +(61) 3 9428 4812
Fax: +(61) 3 9421 1110
Email: craig@rossetti.com.au
Page 178

BRUCE RICKARD & ASSOCIATES
20 Young Street,
Neutral Bay, NSW 2089
Phone: +(61) 2 9908 2811
Fax: +(61) 2 9908 2711
Email: brucerickard@optusnet.com.au
Pages 44 & 92

CRAWFORD ARCHITECTS
378 Abercrombie Street,
Chippendale, NSW 2007
Phone: +(61) 2 9310 5933
Fax: +(61) 2 9310 5944
Email: arch@crawford.com.au
Page 34

CHENCHOW LITTLE ARCHITECTS
422 Bourke Street,
Surry Hills, NSW 2010
Phone: +(61) 2 9357 4333
Fax: +(61) 2 9357 4334
Email: mail@chenchowlittle.com
Page 120

DALE JONES-EVANS
Loft 1, 50–54 Ann Street,
Surry Hills, NSW 2010
Phone: +(61) 2 9211 0626
Fax: +(61) 2 9211 5998
Email: dje@dje.com.au
Pages 22 & 172

DAVID LUCK ARCHITECT
7 Hardy Street,
South Yarra, Vic 3141
Phone/Fax: +(61) 3 9867 7509
Email: david.luck@bigpond.com.au
Page 24

ELIZABETH WATSON BROWN ARCHITECTS
88 Gailey Road Street,
Lucia, Qld 4067
Phone: +(61) 7 3830 7760
Fax: +(61) 7 3830 4752
Email: ebw@eis.net.au
Page 86

DAWSON BROWN ARCHITECTURE
Level 1, 63 William Street,
East Sydney, NSW 2010
Phone: +(61) 2 9360 7977
Fax: +(61) 2 9360 2123
Email: dba@carolinecasey.com.au
Page 60

GREGORY BURGESS ARCHITECTS
10 York Street,
Richmond, Vic 3121
Phone: +(61) 3 9411 0600
Fax: +(61) 3 9411 0699
Email: gba@gregoryburgessarchitects.com.au
Page 142

DESIGN KING COMPANY
795 New South Head Road,
Rose Bay, NSW 2029
Phone: +(61) 2 9371 7392
Fax: +(61) 2 9371 0900
Email: jonking@netspace.net.au
Pages 78 & 134

HOLAN JOUBERT ARCHITECTS
202 Little Page Street,
Middle Park, Vic 3206
Phone: +(61) 3 9696 8140
Fax: +(61) 3 9696 8005
Email: dholan@optusnet.com.au
Pages 98 & 110

DONALDSON + WARN ARCHITECTS
38 Roe Street,
Perth, WA 6000
Phone: +(61) 8 9328 4475
Fax: +(61) 8 9227 6558
Email: admin@donaldsonandwarn.com.au
Page 70

IREDALE PEDERSEN HOOK ARCHITECTS
Suite 26/158 William Street,
Perth, WA 6000
Phone: +(61) 8 9322 8552
Fax: +(61) 8 9322 9752
Email: ipharchs@iinet.net.au
Page 162

DONOVAN HILL ARCHITECTS
112 Bowen Street,
Spring Hill, Qld 4000
Phone: +(61) 7 3831 3255
Fax: +(61) 7 3831 3266
Email: mail@donovanhill.com.au
Page 32

JACKSON CLEMENTS BURROWS ARCHITECTS
1 Harwood Place,
Melbourne, Vic 3000
Phone: +(61) 3 9654 6227
Fax: +(61) 3 9654 6195
Email: jacksonclementsburrows@jcba.com.au
Page 156

EDMISTON JONES ARCHITECTS
49 Bridge Road,
Nowra, NSW 2541
Phone: +(61) 2 4421 6822
Fax: +(61) 2 4422 1963
Email: aej@aej.com.au
Pages 38 & 76

JOHN WARDLE ARCHITECTS
Level 10, 180 Russell Street,
Melbourne, Vic 3000
Phone: +(61) 3 9654 8700
Fax: +(61) 3 9654 8755
Email: johnwardle@johnwardle.com
Page 184

KERSTIN THOMPSON ARCHITECTS
169 Smith Street,
Fitzroy, Vic 3065
Phone: +(61) 3 9419 4969
Fax: +(61) 3 9419 4483
Email: kta@netspace.net.au
Page 108

NEIL & IDLE ARCHITECTS
21 Balmain Street,
Richmond, Vic 3121
Phone: +(61) 3 9428 5600
Fax: +(61) 3 9428 9001
Email: info@neil-idle.com.au
Page 166

LACOSTE + STEVENSON ARCHITECTS
Unit 301/85 William Street,
East Sydney, NSW 2011
Phone: +(61) 2 9360 8633
Fax: +(61) 2 9380 6231
Email: lacoste@cyber.net.au
Page 48

NEVILLE QUARRY ARCHITECT
40 Sir Thomas Mitchell Road,
Bondi, NSW 2026
Phone: +(61) 2 9365 3218
Fax: +(61) 2 9365 3938
Email: quarry@f1.net.au
Page 114

LAHZ NIMMO ARCHITECTS
Level 5, 116–122 Kippax Street,
Surry Hills, NSW 2010
Phone: +(61) 2 9211 1220
Fax: +(61) 2 9211 1554
Email: info@lahznimmo.com
Page 66

NORMAN DAY + ASSOCIATES
Suite 3/15 Inkerman Street,
St Kilda, 3182
Phone: +(61) 3 9534 2144
Fax: +(61) 3 9534 7144
Email: mail@normanday.com
Page 146

MARCUS O'REILLY ARCHITECT
70A Chatsworth Road,
Prahran, Vic 3181
Phone: +(61) 3 9510 6023
Fax: +(61) 3 9510 6053
Email: marcus@marcusoreilly.com
Page 82

ODDEN RODRIGUES ARCHITECTS
Level 1, 267 Stirling Highway,
Claremont, WA 6010
Phone: +(61) 8 9393 3111
Fax: +(61) 8 9385 2439
Email: ora@wantree.com.au
Page 54

MELOCCO & MOORE ARCHITECTS
Level 5/122 Kippax Street,
Surry Hills, NSW 2010
Phone: +(61) 2 9212 6111
Fax: +(61) 2 9212 2050
Email: architects@meloccomoore.com.au
Page 94

PAUL UHLMANN ARCHITECTS
Unit 24/66 Goodwin Terrace,
Burleigh Heads, Qld 4220
Phone: +(61) 7 5576 7321
Fax: +(61) 7 5576 7073
Email: info@pua.com.au
Pages 130 & 136

MOLNAR FREEMAN ARCHITECTS
1/70 Glenmore Road,
Paddington, NSW 2021
Phone: +(61) 2 9356 4680
Fax: +(61) 2 9356 4669
Email: molnarfreeman@bigpond.com.au
Page 104

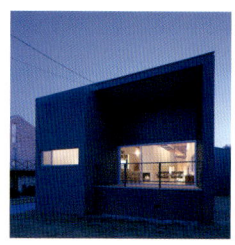

RANDLES HILL STRAATVEIT ARCHITECTS
Level 2/25 Cooper Street,
Surry Hills, NSW 2010
Phone: +(61) 2 9281 8208
Fax: +(61) 2 9212 1716
Email: randleshillstraatveit.com
Page 168

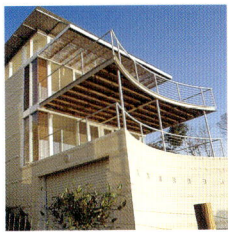

ROBERT CONTI ARCHITECT
Level 1, 174–176 Bouverie Street,
Carlton, Vic 3053
Phone: +(61) 3 9347 2066
Fax: +(61) 3 9347 8981
Email: contiarc@bigpond.com.au
Pages 14 & 150

STUTCHBURY & PAPE ARCHITECTS
4/364 Barrenjoey Road,
Newport, NSW 2106
Phone: +(61) 2 9979 5030
Fax: +(61) 2 9979 5367
Email: snpala@ozemail.com.au
Page 102

ROBERT PULLAR OF ARTICHOKE DESIGN STUDIOS
195 Cape Three Points Road,
Avoca Beach, NSW 2251
Phone: +(61) 2 4382 1463
Fax: +(61) 2 4385 4161
Page 28

SWANEY DRAPER ARCHITECTS
Level 9, 376 Albert Street,
East Melbourne, Vic 3002
Phone: +(61) 3 9417 6162
Fax: +(61) 3 9419 4480
Email: mail@swaneydraper.com.au
Page 126

SAM CRAWFORD ARCHITECT
Level 5, 68–72 Wentworth Avenue
Surry Hills NSW 2010
Phone: +(61) 2 9280 3555
Fax: +(61) 2 9280 3556
Email: samcrawford@ozemail.com.au
Page 72

UTZ-SANBY ARCHITECTS
Suite 101/109 Alexander Street,
Crows Nest, NSW 2065
Phone: +(61) 2 9437 0666
Fax: +(61) 2 9437 0766
Email: utzsanby@ozemail.com.au
Page 152

SJB ARCHITECTS
25 Coventry Road,
Southbank, Vic 3006
Phone: +(61) 3 9699 6688
Fax: +(61) 3 9696 6234
Email: arch@sjb.com.au
Pages 40 & 88

VALDIS MACENS ARCHITECTS
156 Gloucester Street,
Sydney, NSW 2000
Phone: +(61) 2 9241 5799
Fax: +(61) 2 9241 5611
Email: valdismacens@webone.com.au
Page 18

STEPHEN JOLSON ARCHITECT
Studio 1, 251 Chapel Street,
Prahran, Vic 3181
Phone: +(61) 3 9533 7997
Fax: +(61) 3 9533 7978
Email: enquires@sjarchitect.com
Page 174

STEPHEN VARADY ARCHITECTURE
14 Lackey Street,
St Peters, NSW 2044
Phone: +(61) 2 9516 4044
Fax: +(61) 2 9516 4541
Email: svarady@bigpond.com
Page 62

Acknowledgments

I would like to thank all the architects and owners featured in this book. Their dedication in commissioning and designing these magnificent beach houses is clearly expressed in the pages of this book. Thanks must also go to the many photographers who contributed. Their images allow these wonderful beach houses to be enjoyed by all of us. I would also like to thank my partner Naomi for her support and literary criticism.

Some of the work in this book has appeared in *The Age* newspaper, as listed below.

Page 24: 'The End of a Journey' by David Luck Architect, photography by Earl Carter. This house first appeared in Domain, in *The Age* newspaper, on 28 August, 2002.

Page 88: 'The Highest Point' by SJB Architects, photography by Peter Clarke and by Tony Miller. This house first appeared in Domain, in *The Age* newspaper, on 21 January, 2001.

Page 124: 'Maximum Exposure' by Col Bandy Architects, photography by Richard Lenartowicz. This house first appeared in Domain, in *The Age* newspaper, on 31 January, 2001.

Page 126: 'About the Landscape' by Swaney Draper Architects, photography by Trevor Mein. This house first appeared in Domain, in *The Age* newspaper, on 12 February, 2003.

Page 156: 'Robust' by Jackson Clements Burrows Architects, photography by Emma Cross of John Gollings Photography. This house first appeared in Domain, in *The Age* newspaper, on 12 June, 2002.

Page 178: 'Through the Back Door' by Craig Rossetti Architect, photography by Andrew Ashton and by Tim Griffith. This house first appeared in Domain, in *The Age* newspaper, on 5 February, 2003.

Page 180: 'Strategic Incisions' by Brearley Middleton Architects, photography by Erica Lauthier. This house first appeared in Domain, in *The Age* newspaper, on 26 September, 2001.

Every effort has been made to trace the original source of copyright material contained in this book. The publishers would be pleased to hear from copyright holders to rectify any errors or omissions.

The information and illustrations in this publication have been prepared and supplied by the entrants and Stephen Crafti. While all reasonable efforts have been made to source the required information and ensure accuracy, the publishers do not, under any circumstances, accept responsibility for errors, omissions and representations express or implied.